An Indian Spy in Pakistan

An Indian Spy in Pakistan

Mohanlal Bhaskar

Translated by
Jai Ratan

Srishti
PUBLISHERS & DISTRIBUTORS

Srishti Publishers & Distributors
N-16, C. R. Park
New Delhi 110 019
srishtipublishers@gmail.com

First published by
Srishti Publishers & Distrubutors in 2003
Reprinted **2019**

Printed and bound in India

A Night at Sheikh Wahid's

Gulberg has a memorial to Pakistan in the shape of a big minaret, commemorating Qaid-e-Azam Mohammed Ali Jinnah's *Karardad-e-Pakistan* where he had placed a formal proposal before the Muslim League that a separate country should be carved out for the followers of Islam and a resolution was adopted to that effect. Here Muslims would rule independently free from the taint of other religions and consider themselves as 'pure' and 'sacred'. As such the country was named Pakistan – the abode of the pure.

Call it the quirk of history that every sixth house in Gulberg, where that historic resolution was adopted, is now the abode of high-class call-girls. Here also live big shots who have a say in the affairs of Pakistan. Here fates are decided over goblets of wine and at the toss of a pretty head. It is here that aspirants climb up the ladder of administrative hierarchy, sign contracts and obtain route permits and licences.

Someone had taunted the husband of Aklim Akhtar alias General Rani, the keep of Yahya Khan, that did he not feel embarrassed that the General openly hobnobbed with his wife?

The husband smiled, took a sip of whisky and said, "Not at all, Janab. To get on in life I've adopted new ways of thinking. Now I say to myself that this woman is the General's wife and my keep. Once in a while I manage to spend a night with her in bed on the sly."

Sheikh Wahid, tall, with a finely trimmed beard, gold-rimmed spectacles, diamond rings dazzling his fingers, clandestinely dabbled in the business of forged currency notes. Near Adamkhel Pass and in the vicinity of Kair beyond Peshawar, they deal in the currencies of all countries. It is a straightforward business at rates varying from 25 to 50 per cent. Pay with one hand and receive double the amount with the other. The forged notes look so genuine that even banks accept them without raising an eyebrow. One can get all currencies there – the Indian rupee, the American dollar, the Russian rouble. You ask for it and they have it.

To outward appearances, Wahid maintains a guest house which is run by his Begum. I knew its code word. In the morning I had phoned up the Begum. "Madam, I hear these days donkeys too have started eating mangoes," I said. "Really, when did you see them eating mangoes?" she asked. "About six or seven hours ago," I replied. She thanked me and said that she would also like to see these animals. The implication being that she had agreed to my coming over to her place between six and seven in the evening.

I reached her *kothi* at seven on the dot. I gave the *darban* the code word, telling him that I was coming from Adamkhel and had brought grapes. The *darban* immediately threw open the door and let me into the drawing room where the Begum was already waiting to receive me. I stared at her as if looking lost and then taking out Rs. 200 from my pocket placed them on the table before her. She smiled at me as she picked up the money and then pressed a button. The side door opened from which ten dazzling figures emerged, all of them college girls. I stared at them like one bewitched trying to decide whom to select to spend the night with when my mind said that such girls were barren of secrets and a woman like the Begum could only have them. So I sent the girls away.

The Begum gave me a quizzical look.

"I'm sorry Aslam Mian," she said. "These are all the girls that I've tonight. I don't have any other to press into your service." She extended her hand to return my money.

"Please don't stand on niceties," I said. "Tonight I want you."

She looked at me surprised. "You mean you prefer me over those young and beautiful girls?"

I said, "You're not only beautiful in my eyes but also seasoned timber too."

"But I won't be free before ten," she said. "I won't mind waiting," I said. "In the meanwhile you can send me a bottle of whisky."

After finishing my food I was relaxing when the Begum came in. I gaped at her as she stood before me looking like the denizen of some other world. I threw my arms around tier. Perhaps it was after a long time that she had chanced upon a person who really admired her. She opened out to me. Slightly intoxicated, she kept mumbling as she lay in my arms and answered all my questions without demur. About Sheikh Wahid, about the army officers and the places they came from and all the military matters they bragged about.

In the morning I woke up at the muezzin's call. The Begum was still asleep. After taking my bath I looked at the morning's paper. A news item said: "Four rebels shot dead in Lahore Cantonment." I was amazed at this balatant lie. I had myself seen hundreds of people falling under the hail of bullets.

Promising to pay another visit I took leave of the Begum and proceeded towards the Shahnoor Studios which I felt was quite a secure place to spend the day in. Here I came across young boys and girls who had run away from home to try their luck in films. Generally, they are reluctant to tell their correct names and the places they hail from.

From Lahore to Multan

I had to meet someone at Multan Cantt. The bus stand at Lahore looks so bright and gay. And I have liked the bus system of Pakistan. Anybody who has the means can buy a route permit from the government by paying a specified amount and can then ply his bus on this route without any restriction. There is no time schedule and hence there, is a keen competition between bus owners. They vie with each other in attracting a passenger and serving him well. "Come Janab! Come Hazoor! the boys cry as they run after prospective passengers and get a four anna tip per passenger from the bus owner for whom they do the canvassing.

The conductors are equally solicitous of the passengers. The women passengers are taken great care of. If a woman is occupying a seat a man would avoid sitting next to her. The seat would even go vacant till another woman passenger occupies it.

Badami Bagh, the bus station that serves Lahore, is quite big and extensive. It was here that last month two of my spy-friend, Sohanlal and Chanan Singh were put under arrest. In the world of spies such arrests have no special import. They are regarded as a part of the game and are taken in the stride.

Our bus was proceeding towards Kasur and I was specially watchful of the deserted roads whose gaiety had been marred by the martial law. People looked so worried and concerned. They could not openly talk against martial law. As I noticed even now electricity had not reached most of the villages of Pakistan. I bad to get down in a village near Montgomery, where I had to obtain information about some of my acquaintances. I was told that the person concerned would meet me at five in the evening outside the military hospital at Multan. I would be required to wipe my face three times with a red kerchief to establish my identity. I immediately set off for Multan. My guide who was living in this village accompanied me.

We came out of the village and stopped by the roadside, for a bus. In front of us, at the other side of the road there were some passengers waiting for the bus going to Lahore. One of them beckoned me to come over to him and said, "Where are you coming from? And what do you do?" I told him that I was serving as an extra in the Shahnoor Film Company. My answer pleased him and he asked me whom I had come to meet here. "Sheikh Abdul Rahman," I replied. He was startled at my reply. "What do you mean Sheikh Abdul Rahman?" he asked me. My guide at once drew closer to me. "This young fellow has come to meet Sheikh Saheb Din," he said. "He is visiting him for the first time." In the meantime our bus came and saying a hurried good-bye we rushed towards the bus.

"Oh, hell, we had a narrow escape!" my guide whispered in my ear. "That fellow is none other than Sheikh Abdul Rahm an. The Chairman of this place. Even a slight suspicion and you would have got it in the neck."

We reached Khanewal enroute. I got down from the bus and cast a lingering look at the railway cabin room. My grand-father Dadurain bad served as a cabin man at this place. In 1947 he was still here and managed to reach Abohar with great difficulty at the risk of his life.

The bus reached Multan at four in the evening. I left my guide at the bus stand and hired a three-wheeler to take me to the military hospital. At the main gate I took out a red handkerchief from my pocket and wiped my face with it three times. An old man standing at some distance behind me pushed past me. "Mian, get aside," he said, "Why are you blocking my way?" By then a folded piece of paper had slipped into my trouser pocket. I mumbled something as if in objection to his tantrum and after walking a few steps I took a rickshaw and reached the bus stand.

Multan is blazing hot in summer. It is called the city of faquirs. Here lived a faquir by the name of shams-Tabrez, who at the behest of his mentor had flayed his skin and made a gift of it to his mentor. As a result, worms had started crawling over his body. Nobody would even give him alms. One day a butcher took pity on him and threw him a piece of mutton, But nobody was prepared to bake the meat for him. He fixed the chunk of meat on his spear and spreading out his hands in prayer said, "Ya Maula, you, who are the solace of all, if I have worshipped you with a true heart you must come to my rescue." It is said that hearing his supplication, the sun descended so low over the earth that its heat was enough to bake the chunk of meat. This had happened in the twinkling of an eye but the whole city of Multan felt as if it was ablaze. Since that time every year Multan has a blistering summer.

I caught a bus and returned to the same village, Sahiwal, near Montgomery.

At night I called on Sheikh Abdul Rahman. His son, Mohammed Akram, received me very cordially. He evinced keen interest in the film world and the Shahnoor Studios. I tried to satisfy him by telling him a lot of lies. In the morning I left for Lahore.

I straightway made for the Shahdoor Studio where the shooting of 'Jarka', a Pakistani film, which proved to be a great hit was in progress. A dance sequence by Neelo, the heroine of the film was being picturized. Her legs tied with chains, she was lashed as she sang and danced. 'One dies to be born again', she sang. It is the dance of death, a sop to tyranny. 'I will dance on, without a whimper, without bowing my head. For, a lover of freedom can dance even while in chains'.

As I watched the dance I felt it was an oblique reference to the conditions in Pakistan. The entire nation was shackled in chains and dancing to the lashes of martial law. Since its very birth and through its childhood and youth the nation had been ravaged by the martial law fiends whose claws were dripping with the blood of the innocent people. Sometime it was Liaquat Ali and then Iskander Mirza and Ayub. Only the faces changed. But the iron grip of the military hands round the people's neck never relaxed. The film 'Jarka' had been depicting the Palestinian insurgents fighting against the Israelis. It drew an unmistakable parallel with the Pakistani situation.

I was scheduled to leave for Sialkot the following day and spend the night with a friend who had his house not far from the studio. In the morning I met my guide at the Badami Bagh bus stand. Instead of going directly to Sialkot we decided to make a detour to Gujranwala via Lyallpur. Lahore had by then extended up to Lyallpur in the same way as Delhi had stretched upto Rohtak. We took a room in the Grand Hotel at Gujranwala. My guide was an old man of sixty. I told the hotel manager that we were bound for Daska where the old man wanted to have his eyes examined.

Daska is only a few miles from Gujranwala on the Sialkot side and has a reputed eye hospital. After getting my old companion's eyes examined at the hospital and getting the necessary prescription for him, we took the bus to Sialkot. At Danniwala Chowk, a place near Sialkot, a man clad in white got into the bus and sat down by my side. My sixth sense started working, telling me that I must be careful. Getting down at Sialkot we proceeded towards a chemist's shop. On the pretext of cleaning my mercury goggles I looked into the mirror and found the same man standing about fifty yards away from us. He seemed to be keeping a watch over us. Giving up the idea of proceeding towards the Cantonment, we again returned to the bus stand and bought tickets for Daska. The man had also followed us to Daska. But seeing us going towards the eye hospital his suspicion was allayed and he stopped shadowing us.

We spent the night at Gujranwala and proceeded towards Kharian in morning. It is the biggest cantonment in Pakistan, constructed with American aid. The Americans had bestowed this generosity on Pakistan in lieu of obtaining military watch-posts in its territory in order to keep an eye on the Russians. In terms of neatness and layout Kharian is only next to Islamabad.

We were just entering Kharian when we saw a convoy of military vehicles in the distance. We were able to identify it as the First Armoured Corps of Pakistan, apparently returning from military exercises. We asked the bus conductor to extend our tickets upto Jhelum which enabled us to have a full view of the passing convoy. At Jhelum Cantt. we managed to have a close look at the Paton and Shaffe tanks with their 105 mm guns.

We were back to Gujranwala at eight. We stayed in the same hotel for the night and left for Lahore in the morning.

An Alarming News: A Hasty Retreat

My guide Baba Samund Singh alias Imamuddin was an opium addict. Sometimes he was so much gone on it that he would start blubbering or slump down anywhere without warning. But he was a useful man and we went about as father and son. We would buy a buffalo at one place and sell it off at another. If we had to pass through a cantonment we would buy a buffalo in a neighbouring village and get rid of it in one of the villages across the cantonment. In this manner people's attention was diverted towards the animal and they did not take much notice of us. We did not mind any loss in the bargain.

On reaching Lahore the first thing that Samund Singh did was to locate an opium shop where he could replenish his stock. He had only a vague idea of where the thing was sold. Anyway, we hired a taxi and went to Jhandu Shah's 'abode' in Shah Almi. The 'abode' had lost its popularity but still we could see many people hanging around, most of them boozers and hemp-addicts, apart from some innocent lookers-on. Jhandu Shah himself plied a tonga and his 'abode' was run by his wife who reminded me of the hooch-peddling women of Bombay.

Jhandu Shah had not performed regular *nikah* with this woman; she was in fact his keep. Pickpockets and dealers in contraband country liquor, newly initiated into this business enjoyed her active patronage. These young people worked under the nomenclature of 'machines', each I 'machine' having its own individual number and defined area of operation They were strictly forbidden to poach on others' territories. If they wilfully transgressed in this regard there were 'engineers' to bring them to heel. Jhandu Shah was the over-lord of them all. It often happened that a passenger who hired his tonga found his cash and jewellery missing from his box on reaching home. His gang knew a special 'art' which was practised only after nightfall. If a prosperous looking passenger got into his tonga, Jhandu Shah's proteges would materialise from somewhere and get into the tonga. They would engage the unwary passenger in talk, giving Jhandu Shah a free hand to carry out his depredations. On the pretext of taking out his whip from under the Tonga seat he would dexterously break open the lock of the suitcase and in a jiffy pilfer whatever he could conveniently lay his hand upon. He would put the booty in the horse's pouch of grain, carrying out the whole operation with mind-boggling swiftness. Reaching home, when the passenger discovered his loss, he could do nothing else except beat his head in despair. He would think that the theft could have as well taken place on the train.

The police was in regular pay of Jhandu Shah and the officer-incharge of the *thana* had a gay time at his 'abode'. Once Jhandu Shah managed to make a very big haul but he overlooked to share the loot with the DSP Bakar Ali, nick-named Bakre Shah (the he-goat) as a result of which he had Jhandu Shah severely beaten up by half a dozen of his roughs. In the process the DSP was himself exposed but nobody was prepared to run the risk of making any insinuation against him. There are hundreds of such 'abodes' in Lahore and an equally large number of roughs gallivanting around them.

Having got his share of opium, Samund Singh wanted to bide his time somewhere. The curfew had been lifted and I hired a rickshaw to take us to Mohammed Ashraf Butt's house. He was also known as 'Bahnonwalla Butt' – the Butt who boasted of his sisters. He had three beautiful sisters who were hobnobbing with highly placed police officers. A known goonda of the Naulakha area, he also ran a gambling den. He was clever at manipulating cards and fond of *charas* (hemp). As a matter of fact, hemp was very popular in Pakistan. Every sixth man of Lahore was said to be hemp-addict. One could see children of the age of ten and old men of sixty smoking hemp in their cigarettes.

I was on very friendly terms with Butt and could call on him at any odd hour. We spent the night with him and left at nine in the morning. Coming out of the lane we had just stopped at the paan shop to buy *paans* when we heard the radio blaring forth the most alarming news: "Three Indian spies hanged in the Mianwali Jail."

Kapur and his companion Gura, who had been sentenced to death had been languishing in the jail for a long time awaiting their end. I thought that we must immediately leave for India and return at some more propitious time. Our worried looks could give us away.

I spent the day watching the shooting of a film a Bari Studio but my heart was not in it. In the evening we caught the bus at Badami Bagh for Hudiara from where the border was not far.

The call for the evening namaz was on. We leisurely walked towards the Indian border. Our path was flanked by maize fields. We left the path at a lonely spot and hid in a maize field, waiting for the night to advance. After biding our time for two hours we again crept towards the border. We had walked only a few steps when we spotted a live charcoal from which we concluded that one of the Pakistani rangers must have lighted a *chelum* for his *hukkah* and he must be hiding somewhere nearby. It was indeed a tantalising moment for us. How to find out where the fellow was hiding? I ripped off a small piece from Samund Singh's dhoti and twisting it into a thin rope I set a match to its lower end and hung it from a tree. The lower burning portion was only a few inches from the ground. Then we walked for about a hundred yards towards our right and sat down on the ground. As the flame of burning piece of cloth reached a man's height the Pakistani ranger thought that a man waiting to get across the border had lighted a cigarette. He fired in the direction of the burning piece of cloth from which we came to know his exact location. By the time he could run in the direction of the burning cloth we had crossed into the Indian territory.

I am Arrested

It had happened quite some time back. I was staying in Jalandhar when at about eight at night someone knocked on my door. A hefty man, more than six feet tall, was standing outside the door, along with one of my companions. My companion introduced him as Amrik Singh. He told me he was one of us, having similar pursuits as ours. There were orders from the higher-ups to lodge him with me for the night as he had to leave for Pakistan the following morning. Although I arranged for a charpoy for the newcomer, my sixth sense for some unknown reason had already started troubling me. Something told me that this man could not be depended upon. After sometime I decided to test him. Leaving my bag near my bed, I told him that I was going to the toilet. Purposely I did not switch on the verandah light. I proceeded towards the toilet, noisily closed its door and then taking off my shoes tiptoed back to my room. The verandah was dark and he could not see me. I saw through a chink in the door that the man had taken out the papers from my bag and after a hurried glance at them was putting them back in the same order. My suspicion was confirmed. I went back to the toilet, put on my shoes and returned, clip-clapping my shoes. I could not sleep the whole night.

It was raining hard in the morning. I had to go out for my breakfast but I was not prepared to leave Amrik Singh alone in my room at any cost. I asked him to come with me. But he objected to going out in that heavy rain but I brushed aside his objection. I told my officer about my experience with the man. When the officer questioned him he took the matter lightly and denied everything. He had a way of allaying suspicion.

Four months later, when I started from home on the morning of 16th Sept., 1968 all sorts of ugly thoughts assailed my mind. I felt like jumping down from the running train and return home. But fate had ordained differently. Next day I reached the check-post of Khatra from where I had to cross the border in the afternoon. I heard the following song being sung over the Akashvani : *O, janewaley ho sakey to lautke ana* (O, wayfarer, there's still time for you to return).

In the last couple of months four of my companions had been arrested while spying in Pakistan and I felt that the song was a premonition of what was coming to me. Even so, when the moon waned at two, as if involuntarily tied by the threads of duty I stepped across the border. This time my feet lacked the previous agility and something seemed to have sapped my determination. I had hardly crossed the border when an owl screeched and my heart sank. There were still three hours for the morning to arrive. I spread a bedsheet in a maize field and went to sleep. My guide, Baba Samund Singh alias Imamudin was also with me. He had taken an opium pill and dozed off immediately but I failed to get any sleep. In the dark I saw unknown hands advancing towards my neck. The muezzin gave the call for the morning namaz. We got up, washed our faces in the nearby pond and took to the road.

We had already traversed eight miles into Pakistan. The morning was already upon us and in this broad daylight there was no question of going back to India. The bus was ready to start for Lahore. We got into it but my mind was in turmoil. On this side of Barki, there is a small Village by the roadside known as Chhota Barka. When the bus stopped there I saw Amrik Singh of all persons entering it. There were four people along with him. He exchanged greetings with me and sat down in the seat next to me. My heart had started pounding hard and my breath seemed to have stuck in my throat. I had a foreboding of something terrible in the offing. When the bus was crossing over the Ichogil Canal, avoiding others' attention I threw my minicamera into the canal. Some unknown power had induced me to do so.

After a few miles the bus stopped at a rail crossing. I got down from the bus and walking leisurely stopped in front of the gate of the rail crossing. A train was due to pass. I thought of crossing over to the other side and waited to time the move.

But it only remained a pious wish. Then I found Amrik Singh standing by my side. "Jameel (Amrik Singh's assumed Pakistani name), who are these people with you?" I asked him. "You fool, don't you know?" he guffawed. "They are my smuggler friends." Then he quickly added, "You fool, why have you turned pale? You must compose yourself. Otherwise you will give away the game. We shall get ditched along with you."

But somehow I felt that his laugh was hollow and his talk nothing but simulation. But I was helpless. There was no way of escape. Pistols were peeping out from the waists of his friends whereas I was defenceless.

My condition was that of a goat being dragged by the butcher to be slaughtered. Perhaps even worse. I could not even bleat like a goat.

As we got down from the bus Amrik Sinkh turned to my guide, "Baba, your thing is safe with me. I'll give it back to you when you are taking your tea."

He took us to the Zamindara Hotel in Lahore. His companions were still with him. Then I suddenly thought of a ruse. I asked the hotel man to boil two *seers* of milk for us. I thought I would throw the scalding milk in the faces of my tormentors and escape in the confusion. A man scalded with boiling milk takes at least half an hour to recover.

The milk was placed on the oven to boil. But it seemed that the dice was heavily loaded against me.

Amrik Singh suddenly left the room on the plea of getting

a packet of cigarettes. "I'll be back in a minute," he said, giving me a meaningful look.

As soon as he was gone one of his comparmons exclaimed, "Hands up!" and I found a pistol menacingly held against my chest.

"Who are you?" he asked me

"Mohammed Aslam," I replied.

"Where do you live?"

"Sahiwal. Chak No. 7."

"Who's the Chairman of that place?"

"Sheikh Abdul Rahman."

"What do you do for a living?"

"I sell buffaloes."

"Where am you coming from?"

"From Sarja Mirza."

"All right, we shall take you to our office. If you are really a Pakistani we shall let you off."

They tied my hands behind my back and took me in a taxi to Lahore Cantonment. When the taxi took a turn a Subedar among them said to me. "Well Mister Mohan Lal Bhaskar B.A. B.Ed. we are taking you to 78, Nalwa Road, Jalandhar Cantt. where you have your office."

Now there was no scope for any doubt in my mind. The worst had already happened.

I was mentally preparing myself for the trouble that Jay in store for me. The taxi stopped. The cloth was removed from my eyes. We had arrived at our destination. Previously I had scores of times passed by the 596 Field Interrogation Unit. It was located in a building about two furlongs from the airfield, with armed guards posted at both its entrances. Passing through a dark corridor I was halted before a room at whose door a red lamp was burning. The peon sent word inside. I was ushered into the presence of Major Aijaz Maqsood, a handsome, well-built, young man. He signalled me to sit down in a chair. The peon had already removed my handcuffs.

The Major offered me tea and then started interrogating me. "Mr. Bhaskar, you are educated and you have hardly been married for a year. You know, of course, that it is a hazardous profession and death can snatch you away anytime. May I know what made you to opt for this line of activity?"

I don't know what mysterious power was prompting me to speak in the manner that I did. I was myself amazed at what I said in reply. I said, "The day of death is fixed, Major Saheb. You have love for your country. So you can understand it better."

For an instant he found himself in a quandary. But he recovered quickly and sighed, "Why are you being cruel to yourself," he said "I swear by Quran-i-Karim, if you give me correct answers I'll release you immediately and promise you safe conduct back to your country. You fool, I feel sorry for your youth. Only tell me who passed on to you that file relating to the Atomic Energy? It was given to you at Islamabad, if I'm not mistaken."

"Atomic Energy Commission, Islamabad," I mumbled to myself under my breath. "Excuse me, Major Saheb," I said. "I've received no such file. Perhaps you're labouring under some misapprehension."

I had hardly finished speaking when he kicked me hard. I fell headlong, the chair I was sitting in toppling over me. The cup of tea I was holding in my hand flew in the air and struck against the wall. The Major's face tingled with rage. "I'm taking pity on you and you're trying to fool me. Foolish man, your companion Amrik Singh has told us everything. You paid Rs. 13,000 for a file relating to the Atomic Energy Commission, Islamabad, and sent it on to India. And now you have the cheek to say that you know nothing about it."

"Major Saheb, how can an educated man like you ever think that any file relating to the Energy Commission can fall into alien hands?" I replied wiping the blood from my mouth. "If such a thing could happen then uranium could also disappear from there. And so could plutonium. No, Major Saheb, you're wrongly informed."

"Don't think I'm a kid. We had checked our stock the moment we got the news. If you had not been caught even such an eventuality was within the pale of possibility. If we can buy your Amrik Singh can't you people buy one of our men? In such a big Organisation one could always find a man willing to join hands with the enemy. Never mind, now you use all your ingenuity to hide your secrets and we shall on our part pulverise your bones, if need be, to extract those secrets from those bones. There are always two at a game."

He rang the bell. "Take him away," he said to the guard. "Take him to Havaldar Aziz and tell him to work on his body right and proper. Bring I him back to me when he's ready to open his mouth."

Havaldar Aziz, fairly young, going by his looks, was a resident of Rawalpindi. He stripped me of all my clothes and asked me to lie down on my face. Then he had a thick branch cut down from a tree standing in the compound. Its knots had not been smoothened out. He sent for two jawans and asked one of them to hold down my legs and the other to sit astride my back. The session of torture had begun. As the knotted part of the branch struck against my body it drew blood from it. The small cell where I was lying was filled with my shrieks. They continued beating me for one and a half hours but to no avail.

I did not tell them a word more than what Amrik Singh had already told them. I refused to confess that I knew anything about the Atomic Energy file. My consciousness was now slowly ebbing away. My eyes drooped and started closing. Suddenly darkness swam before my eyes. I had passed out.

When I came after an hour I found myself lying in a narrow room, no more than six feet long, three feet wide and six feet high. Outside it was an iron railing and beyond it a wooden door. In the middle of the door they had cut out a four inch wide aperture through which a sentry's eyes and a bayonet were peeping in. Somewhere near me I also heard Baba Samund Singh's harrowing shrieks. It appeared as if four or five people were busy beating him. After some time his shrieks ceased.

There was a knock on my door. The guard had come to fetch me. One gunman tightly handcuffed my hands at my back. When I came out I saw a sight which made my flesh creep. Baba Samund Singh was hanging upside down from a rope and had fainted. On my reaching there he was taken down and laid down on the ground. Major Aijaz was present there, blithely puffing away at a cigarette. He gave me a sarcastic smile. "Hi, patriot! Son, the game is on. We shall see how long your patriotism lasts out. You seem to be hell bent upon sacrificing your life. Never mind, I'm the last person to show you any compassion."

I had no answer to what he had said. Moreover, I was in no condition to make an attempt I was again stripped off my clothes and made to stand on a table. My hands were tied to a rope hanging from the wall at my back. The rope passed through a pulley under the ceiling. Then the table was whisked away from under my feet and I was left suspended in the air. The rope cut through my wrists. The rope does not hurt a lean man so much as a fat man. Even so, when hung in this manner even a study man cannot remain in his senses for Lahore than fifteen minutes.

Now a couple of jawans started beating me, each of them having a rod to beat me with. Subedar Anwar Khan who had an inch thick cane was in the lead. He struck the cane against the soles of my feet while Subedar Mohammed Aslam took care of my legs. Havaidar Aziz had a flat washing rod which time and again fell heavily against my waist. Not to be outdone, another man, Naik Noor Khan was pummeling my back with a stick. Major Aijaz Maqsood was also very much in the picture. He was 'lovingly' caressing my head with a thin mulberry cane. All this while two jawans were handling the rope. As the rope went up my screams became louder. Then my body lost the sensation of pain. I was past the feeling that I was being beaten. I was gradually getting into a faint. I had even stopped struggling for I had realised that by doing so the rope was cutting deeper into my wrists. At last I let my body sag as if I did not exist. A peaceful sleep started creeping over my mind. Major Aijaz splashed a jugful of water over my face. "Son, you can be allowed to die here but not sleep," he said. I asked for some water. The Major laughed. "So you want water?" he said. "Water for you who have come to wage a *jehad* against us? But remember we did not give water even to the grandsons of the holy Prophet Rasul-e-Karim on the battle-field of Karbala. Why are you profaning your path to martyrdom by asking for water?"

I don't know what happened next. I had completely passed out by that time. When I came to I again found myself lying in a narrow dungeon like room. In the sun filtering through the aperture in the door I could see the shadow of a bayonet falling over my body. I wondered how long I would be living under its shadow. It was just the beginning of a long life of torment. Every fibre of my body was aching, for there was no part of my body which had been spared a beating. Being the only child of my parents I had lived a pampered life and had not even known the meaning of a slap. Being a promising student in the class I had not known the taste of caning either. And as for the college, the question of corporal punishment did not arise. I did not know for which sin of mine I was now being punished in such a gruesome manner.

The wooden door creaked open and the cook came in with the food – *daal* and four chapatis baked in a *tandoor* (oven). The unit's kitchen was close by. I was also given a plate, a mug and a bowl. I tried to raise my hand to receive the chapatis but it refused to oblige; I just couldn't raise my hands. The sentry ran out and reported the matter to the guard Commander. He came and had my hands massaged. "He'll be all right in a minute," he said. "This happens when a man is hung from a rope." True enough, after a little more massaging my hands started working.

I had gone without food since morning and fell to eating ravenously. The enquiry office had closed for the day and there was nobody about. The Guard Commander Karamat Ali came in and patted my back and *said,* "*Shabash,* don't lose heart. Only the brave suffer. Remember your God in whom you have faith. Allah has given you time to pray. Our Hazrat Usuf-ul-Islam remained in prison for forty years. He had prayed so intensely that when he was released from prison even its walls wept for now they would no more be hearing the sacred word. Only those whom Allah loves undergo privations and suffering. I'm a syyed by caste and your forehead tells me that Allah has brought you here for some higher purpose. Resign yourself to your lot and abide by His will. Eat well. If you remain alive, *Insha Allah,* one day you'll join your wife and children."

At the mention of my family the chapati fell from my hand and my eyes filled with tears. I said, "Pir Saheb, I haven't been married even for one year. My child is still in my wife's womb, five months gone. I don't know how she will bear this shock and how my aged parents will stand this separation. I am their only child. *Hai,* I can't even send any news to them." I started sobbing.

Karamat Ali said, "Don't be a fool. Why do you cry for

them? They are free and can console one another. But you have no one here to stand by you. You must take care of yourself. You have no idea what kind of fate awaits you. I know about my countrymen. They are not like me. I know you're an enemy of our country but I'm taking to you in the name of humanity, although I'm forbidden to do so. Our Major Sabeb is not a bad sort. If you cooperate with him your punishment can be diluted. Anyway I'm not concerned with such matters of higher import. You are capable of thinking what is good and what is bad for you. My job is to keep a watch on you. Here, I've some fruit for you." He placed a quarter *seer* of grapes in my hand. "Don't be surprised," be said. "You'll get your rations from our unit. According to the regulations you are entitled to what the jawans get. The urine bottle is lying inside. The sweeper will empty it in the morning. As for your 'bigger' job and bath, you'll be taken out from this cell in the morning. All right, *shab-e-khair* (good night) I must go. It's time for my namaz."

Then he addressed the sentry, "Sakhi Mohammed, take care of him. Give him water if be asks for it. This man is suffering because of his own doings. He is responsible for it, not we. After your duty is over Lai Khan will take over from you. Pass on my instructions to him." He to go and then stopped. "Keep the outer wooden door open. *Shab-e-khairt"*

Karamat Ali was gone, leaving me pleasantly surprised at his kind behaviour. He was really an angel to me. His words kept ringing in my ears.

After finishing my meal my eyes became heavy with sleep. I asked the sentry to fill my mug with water so that I should not bother him at night. The image of my wife and my parents kept revolving before my eyes. I spread a blanket on the floor and rolling up the other into a pillow, I stretched myself on the blanket. I felt as if I was resting after performing a thousand-mile journey. The muezzin gave the call for the night's namaz. And then I slid into the lap of sleep.

At mid-night my sleep was disturbed by a human cry and I came awake. It appeared as if someone was cutting a goat's throat with a sharp knife. My heart started pounding hard. It was not Samund Singh's voice. Perhaps it was some other Man spy or a suspect. And then to my utter surprise, the victim had started abusing his tormentors.

The guard Sakhi Mohammed had left and I guessed it must be Lal Khan who had taken over from him. "Who is being tortured?" I asked him. He placed his finger on his lips, admonishing me to keep quiet. At the other end, the process of torture was in full swing. As they went at him he responded with the filthiest of abuses. "I'll mount over your mothers, sisters and wives! *Haramis*, sons of bitches!" It appeared he had gone mad and was raving. Or he was trying to commit suicide. I knew they would kill him in the end.

Then his shrieks became fainter and changed into groans, followed by a rattling sound emerging from his throat. I couldn't make out what they were doing to him now. Perhaps he had been placed in an electric chair and was being given an electric shock. Would I also get my turn at the chair? Then I heard the rattling of chains. Perhaps they were dragging a mountain-like heavy man towards some cell. The guard quickly closed the wooden door of my cell which prevented me from seeing the expression on his face. But this man did not belong to my group. None from our group was so hefty and tall. Perhaps he was an army officer. But who was he? He was still abusing his tormentors. At last they clapped him into a cell and departed. I felt relieved. They seemed to have spared me for the time being.

The guard again opened the wooden door of my cell. "Don't ever talk to me in their presence," he said. "It's strictly forbidden." I nodded my head in acknowledgement. "He's one of your Hindustani brethren," the guard continued. "He is here for the last two months but they have not even been able to find out his name. "They torture him every night and are thoroughly fed up with him. The junior officers want to put a bullet into his head but the senior officers would have none of it. Because of the accord between the two countries such a thing cannot be done."

I felt reassured. Under any circumstances they would not shoot me dead. But what about torture? How long would they continue to torture me? Surely, this ordeal was bound to come to an end one day. But would it really? Or it would continue for ever? Couldn't some mysterious power that had come to the rescue of Prahlad, saving him from the leaping flames, or had saved Yusuf from the belly of a fish, also come to my help? Stories from the Hindu mythology leapt to my mind, steeling my mind against the impending disaster.

Since you reside within me,

In every fibre of my body,

In my blood, in my veins,

Who will suffer if they torture me?

Not I -You, only you!

So why this unnecessary worry?

This plight of mine, I told myself, was like a bad dream which would be shattered as soon as I woke up. Consoled by such thoughts I again dozed off.

In the morning as the birds started chirping, our cells were opened and we were led out to answer the call of nature and have our baths. We were, of course, blind-folded and our hands were tied at our backs, the guards close at our heels. After we had finished, we were again confined to our cells. Then the breakfast came – mug of hot tea, two *puris* and *halva*. *I* was going to eat when the guard Sakhi Mohanuned stopped me. "Don't overeat," he warned me. "If they take you away for interrogation it will cause you discomfort." Acting on his advice, I contended myself with tea and a bite or two at a *puri*. The rest of the food was taken away by the sweeper. The wooden door was again closed upon me.

I heard the movement of motor vehicles. I knew what was coming. It must be my tormentors. I didn't have to wait for more than an hour. There was a flurry of activity outside my cell. The door burst open and the guard clicked his boots in attention. I saw Major Aijaz entering the cell.

"Any complaints about the food?"

"No, Janab."

"Did you sleep well?"

"Yes, Janab, I had a sound sleep."

"I've instructed Anwar Saheb to record your statement. I don't believe in wanton cruelty. It's upto you how you record your statement but don't try to conceal anything. I've told you. It may prove your undoing. Nobody is going to touch you today. We know everything about you and you are fully aware of this fact. So try to be sensible."

The Major departed. The door of the cell again closed upon me. I heaved a sigh of relief.

Khoh Singh: Son of Faisla Singh

When a man is temporarily relieved of his worries his thoughts turn to others. The last night's scene revolved before my eyes. How mercilessly they were beating that Indian. But who was be? Having nothing to do I was indulging in idle thoughts. Major Aijaz had assured me that nobody was going to harass me that day. But the door opened and I found that the guard had come to fetch me. Perhaps they wanted to record my statement. They blind-folded me and tied my hands at my back. Then they led me out, a man with a gun in front and another behind me. The havaldar was walking by my side, holding my arm. I suddenly laughed. I recalled having seen in a film King Poras being presented before Alexander in the same manner.

We entered a room. The cloth was removed from my eyes. Subedar Anwar was sitting at a table before me. He was very polite to me. "Did you sleep well?" he asked. "Yes, I slept all right. But at midnight I heard someone screaming and it disturbed my sleep." The Subedar smiled. "I hope you will take a lesson from that and record your statement faithfully without any fabrication. Otherwise you know what's going to happen to you. You will meet a similar fate as that man. I don't know what clay that man is made of. We have been beating him regularly for the last two months but he refuses to open his mouth. We have tried all sorts of devices but none of them has worked on that son of an owl. He eats sixteen *puris* at breakfast. And if you refuse he abuses you right and left. He says, "Sala, if you beat me so mercilessly at least feed me well in return." The fool is thoughtlessly adding to his troubles. If he wants to rot here, let him for all we care. It is of his own making. He should know that the sooner he makes his statement the sooner he will be relieved of his misery. Anyway, now out with your statement!"

I was careful to repeat what I thought Amrik Singh had told them about me. After recording my statement be looked up at me. "What about the Atomic Energy Commission?" he asked. "You're again slurring over this important fact. Well, it's entirely upto you. I can see that you are bent upon committing a folly. You'll suffer for it, for sure. Major Saheb asked me to leave you alone. Otherwise I would have put your cleverness to the test." He rang the bell for the guard and asked him to take me back to my cell. I took my afternoon meal and went to sleep. And then the night descended upon me. Sakhi Mohammed was on duty that night. When he came I salaamed him: immediately came. He smiled and asked me how I was getting along. When I alluded to Khoh Singh he out of his shell. "A wonderful man," he said. "I've not seen the like of him in my whole life. It was about two months back when he first met our jawans at Khare Peron near Kasur. He had a most overbearing personality and they dared not accost him. In fact it was he who accosted them first. "O, jawan, where am you going?" he asked. "Janab, we are out on patrol duty," they replied. "But who are you?" "Don't you know me?" he looked at them in surprise. "I'm the new Thana Incharge of Kasur, I've taken charge just this morning." And then he walked away.

It had, however, aroused the jawans' suspicion and they reported the matter to their JCO who went in chase of the fellow in his jeep. He was waiting for a bus by the roadside when the JCO caught up with him. He respectfully asked the man to get into the jeep for his Major Saheb wanted to have the pleasure of meeting the new Thana Officer. In the meantime the Major had ascertained that no new incumbent had been posted at Kasur as Thana Incharge. The moment the man was presented before the Major he was hung from a rope. Since then this man has been feigning madness. Before he was caught he spoke English but now he professes that he is innocent of it. All the time be keeps saying, "I'm a *pahalwan* living near the border and get by force, whatever I want to eat. My name is Khoh Singh and my father's Faisla Singh." You must have seen the terrible condition he is in. What you saw last night has been happening with him for the last two months. But be opens his mouth only to talk filth and not a word more. When he wants to light a cigarette or wants a drink of water, the *sala* calls the sentry, addressing him as the specimen of a degenerate nation. I feel like putting a bullet through his head but I'm helpless."

We were still talking about Khoh Singh when we heard him calling out to the guard. "You son of a bullet," he cried. "If you want to do justice to your mother's milk just hand me your gun for a minute. And then if I don't put your battalion on the run right from Lahore down to Karachi and drown it in the Gulf of Kutch I'm not Khoh Singh!"

"O, *bhahi*, you're only inviting trouble by talking such rubbish," I shouted out to Khoh Singh from my cell. "Why can't you hold your peace?"

"Shut up, you!" he shouted back at me. "*Sala*, who are you to interfere in my affairs? It's my in-law's place. I've the right to abuse them. These bloody scoundrels! Whom else will I abuse if not them?"

A jeep entered the compound. It appeared his 'lovers' had come. When they opened the door to take him out he glared at them balefully.

"This time you seemed to have remembered your sister's husband a bit too early. Go away, you *salas*! Allow me to sleep in peace for some time more.

Subedar Anwar Khan said, "Son, today we are going to put

you to your eternal sleep. You'll be mounting the gallows."

"Listen, you filthy specimens of a degraded nation! I've not come here to mount the gallows but your sister. Bring me your sister."

"Gag his bloody mouth!" the Subedar thundered. "Put him in the jeep! Today I'm going to take him to the border and shoot him dead."

Eight people rushed upon him while the Subedar struggled to gag his mouth with a piece of cloth.

I kept waiting for his return for three hours. But he did not return.

And then I fell asleep.

In the Naulakha Police Station at Lahore

In their effort to extract the Atomic Energy secret from me the intensity of my torture was mounting from day to day. But it served no purpose. They gave me an electric shock, treated my body with chilli powder, made me lie down on slabs of ice third degree methods continued relentlessly.

One, day the outer door of my cell opened. Four men entered and asked me to collect my things. They blindfolded and handcuffed me at my back. Samund Singh was also taken out of his cell. Where were they taking us? To some other torture chamber?

I was pushed into the front seat of a jeep. From the noise on the road I could make out that we were passing through a crowded bazaar. The jeep stopped after driving for about twenty minutes. The bandage was removed from my eyes and I found myself standing at a police station in Lahore. Chaudhri Nisar Ahmed, a police Sub-Inspector, before whom we were presented was an elderly man. He asked a havaldar to chargesheet me with unlawful entry into Pakistan and in addition under 29 DPR and Section 3 of the Official Secrets Act and 59 Army Act of Pakistan. The whole procedure was conducted under his supervision.

After that we were searched and put in the lock-up in the company of ordinary Pakistani criminals.

The winter had started and we were given blankets, each to be shared by two persons. We were not given any food. The Pakistani prisoners, out of sheer compassion gave us some of their food which they had been able to get from their homes. After a month of torture it was for the first time that I felt free from mental tension. The Pakistani people are very fond of Indian songs. At their insistence, I reeled out four songs, one after the other. Even the sentry on duty leaned forward lending his ear to listen. He brought me a cup of tea which I shared with Samund Singh.

It was going on to be ten and the sentry brought the singing session to a close. Then we had a round of storytelling. Two of the prisoners among us were good storytellers and we heard them with rapt attention, even though if narrated at some other occasion they would be found to be devoid of any merit. I fell asleep and woke up only when the sweeper called. He had come to sweep the place. The water-carrier filled the pitchers and we went to a corner, one by one, to ease ourselves. The sweeper carried away the excreta. Nothing was served for the breakfast.

At ten I and Samund Singh were called out by out names.

The guard had come to carry us to the court where we were taken on a tonga. We were passing through picturesque bazaars. But the policemen who were escorting us to the court were manifestly unhappy. They had lost their extra daily earnings because of us. Had we been some ordinary Pakistani prisoners money would have readily changed hands and the policemen would have got excellent food to boot. We reached the court and were shoved into the presence of the magistrate, Irshad Ali Shah who put us under remand for three days.

They got us food, from a *dhaba* – a cheap wayside eating place. Two *rotis* each and a free helping of *daal*. In all it had cost them four annas per head. People were curious to draw us into conversation but the guards would have none of it. Then we were put on a local bus and brought back to Naulakha. Chaudhri Nisar had been entrusted with the responsibility of investigating our cases. The Lahore police is notorious for its cruelty and high-handedness. It could inflict most atrocious tortures. I think now I lived only to eat and to be beaten. It had become a rigid pattern of my life and ironically, it was upto me to make the best of it. I could spend the day smiling or singing.

At four we were again taken out of our cell and presented before Chaudhri Nisar. He proceeded with his questions in a leisurely manner. When I told him that I was the son of police constable Pandit Amin Chand who had before the partition served with the traffic police and then at the time of partition had gone to Abohar where Mian Sarvar was the Incharge, Chaudhri's eyebrows went up in surprise. "So you are that black Bratunin's son ?" he exclaimed. He beat his head in despair. "You fool, why have you been so cruel to yourself? Do you know under what travails he had managed to get you? You were born to his second wife. Eight years after his second marriage. During this period your parents had knocked at the shrines of every *pir* and *sadhu*. Once they had gone bare foot in the blazing sun to the mausoleum of Panj Pir at Abohar where they were given a talisman and the presiding man there prayed for your birth. You were born during the Second World War and your parents had celebrated your arrival with great eclat. The big-wigs of Abohar had visited your house – Rai Saheb Kundan Lal Ahuja, Darbari Lal Narang, Mian Sarvar – I've forgotten the other names. I had myself been invited to the party. The pir had said that after you, your parents won't have another child. Have you got a brother or sister?"

"No, Chaudhri Saheb, I've a step-sister from father's other wife."

Chaudhri Saheb shook his head dolefully and asked a policeman to bring tea and sweets. He gave the money from his own pocket.

"My dear boy, I can't be of much help to you," he said. "Your crime is such that I cannot endanger my life for your sake. I can't even inform your father. You will be here for a fortnight or so and I'll see to it that no harm is done to you during this period. Here an enquiry is just a formality. You are coming here from a very important centre. The place has no importance as compared to that."

"Where will they send me from this place?" I asked him.

"My boy, I wish I knew. You have ruined your life and your father's too. I am really sorry for it. Your father used to be a very jovial person. Strong and hefty and tall, who could strike terror in a criminal's heart. I am talking of the British regime when a policeman could bring an entire village to his heels, single-handed. What made you get entangled in this dirty morass? My hands are tied. I'm sorry for that. But had you been a Pakistani I would have seen to it that you got away with impunity even if you had committed a murder. But spying is considered to be a dirty game. All that I can do is to pray for you. May Allah have mercy on you. I've called the barber. Have a shave and take a bath."

I was deeply touched and my eyes brimmed with tears. Reverentially, I touched his feet and said, "Chachaji (uncle), fate plays a crucial role in man's life. There could have been a cruel man in your place. Mysterious are the ways of God. On the one hand he has dragged me into this morass and on the other hand he has brought noble souls such as you and Syyed Karamat Ali Shah into my life."

Chaudhri Nisar said, "Don't blame Allah for it. It's your

own misdeeds whose fruits you are reaping now. It's your mother's, father's and wife's prayers that have so far steered you away from the ultimate calamity."

I wished I could bring the Hindu fanatics to show them that even among the Muslims there are pious souls whom they do not know and do not hesitate even to regard them as their worst enemies. Such souls are even nobler than angels. Nobody knows how long these walls of hatred will stand between the Hindus and the Muslims. It is the doing of the Pandits and Mullahs who disgorge their venom through vicious propaganda. The leaders of RSS and the Muslim League inflame our passions in order to hold on to their seat of power.

I was kept in the Naulakha Police Station for about a fortnight. Then the magistrate ordered us to be sent to the Kot Lakhpat Jail at Lahore. While I was leaving Naulakha Police Station Chaudhri Nisar came to me and said, "May Allah be with you, my boy. Don't lose heart. Allah will set everything right." He fondled my head. I saw that his eyes had filled with tears.

The tonga started on its journey. I was passing through the bazaars of Lahore with tear-dimmed eyes. I felt as if there was no enemy around. As if everybody was like me – a part of myself. The word 'enemy' seemed to have lost its relevance.

We caught a bus at Chauburji and reached Kot Lakhpat Jail

which was situated in a lonely place amidst the farms. A big gate opened and we were produced before the Superintendent, Haji Iftkhar, who ordered us to be lodged in a death cell, where only such prisoners, as had been sentenced to death, were kept. It had been done as a precaution to prevent us from meeting other Pakistani prisoners.

Kot Lakhpat Jail, Lahore

Many great men have known prison life. Either their practical lives began in a prison or ended in it. A prison is no less than a university, where one learns so many secrets of life. Here one also meets all sorts of persons who have acquired questionable skills-pickpockets, gamblers, distillers of hooch, house-breakers, dacoits, embezzlers, who rub shoulders with musicians, poets, statesmen, spiritual leaders and philosophers. Now I had entered the portals of one such university. I was taken to its central office, popularly known as the 'circle', for all the barracks of the jail take off from this central point. Here the educated prisoners work as clerks.

Just as in a university the new entrants have to submit themselves to ragging, here also a new prisoner is greeted with a 'salaam'. Only such prisoners who have a big stake in the world of crime or are hardened ones escape this 'salaam' which can be both mild and rigorous. When I entered into the Central Office the clerks raised their heads and gave me contemptuous looks. "So you are a spy?" one of them said in a derisive tone.

"No, Janab......"

"O, come off it. Your mother......" he gave me a filthy abuse. He had hardly uttered these words when someone threw a blanket upon us from behind and giving us a push pinned us down to the ground. After that we lost count of the blows that were showered upon us by innumerable hands.

Their jeerings and our shrieks drew the warder's attention who probably came down running and asked them to stop this hideous game. All this was so sudden and unexpected that we had hardly anytime to prepare ourselves mentally or physically to face this onslaught.

At last the wardens pushed us into the death cells. Four cells in a corner had been earmarked for Indian prisoners in which thirteen prisoners were already lodged, at the rate of three to five persons per cell. Kot Lakhpat is a newly constructed jail which boasts of taps and flush latrines. Here I met six of my companions who had been arrested through the nefarious machinations of Amrik Singh – Sohanlal from Adampur, Chanan Singh Bhuller from Ferozpur and Ajit Singh, among others. I was kept in a separate cell from them.

The jail food was very interior. We were given two *rotis* and a ladleful of *daal*. In the morning we were doled out a handfulof parched gram and a piece of *gur*. As for tea, it was anything but tea. In a month we were given the fourth part of a cube of soap to wash our clothes with. And every Sunday a spoonful of oil to apply to our hair. We were strictly forbidden to go near the rooms of Pakistani prisoners.

It was my second day in the Kot Lakhpat Jail when I woke up in the night on hearing some eerie sounds. Then the entire jail started resounding with the cries of 'Inquilab Zindabad! People's Party Zindabad! Quaid-e-Azam Zindabad! Ayub Shai Murdabad!' The prisoners were responding to these slogans from within their rooms and furiously banging on their doors, asking to be let out. The railings outside their rooms rattled as the prisoners tried to uproot them. The news had spread in the jail that Bhutto Saheb had been brought there under arrest along with his companions.

The situation was taking an ugly turn and it was feared that soon it would get out of control. But the Superintendent was a seasoned man who knew all the ropes. "I appeal to the prisoners to remain calm," he announced over the public address system. "Tomorrow morning I will arrange your meeting with your beloved Bhutto Saheb. Meanwhile, he has something to tell you. I'm passing on the mike to him."

The entire jail suddenly lapsed into silence. Not even a leaf stirred. Then we heard Bhutto Saheb's voice: "Aslam-ulekam! I am myself keen to meet you and I am grateful for the respect and honour that you have bestowed upon me. But what you want is not possible at this juncture. We would not like to jeopardise the interest of the jail authorities who are only carrying out their duties. We do not want to endanger their jobs. God willing, I shall certainly meet you in the morning. I would plead with you to hold your peace till then. I hope you will pay heed to my request. Pakistan Zindabad!"

The Jail Superintendent had very cleverly saved the situation, otherwise it could have led to great bloodshed. Nobody had a wink of sleep that night. The nambardars told us that Bhutto Saheb, Qauser Niazi, Ghulam Mustafa Khar and other leaders of the People's Party who had been brought to the jail under arrest would make a round of the barracks in the morning. We were all waiting for the moment when we would be able to have a glimpse of this great personage who had shaken the very foundations of the military regime and kindled the spark of democracy in the hearts of the people of Pakistan. Ultimately, the man who was regarded is the messiah of the people was most outrageously sent to die gallows by Zil-ul-Haq while the people had watched it happen with a surge of important rage. Just as the murder of Gandhi had tarnished the name of the Hindus forever, in the same way the Pakistanis will not be able to wash off the blood of Bhutto from their foreheads.

The barracks started resounding with slogans which meant that Bhutto Saheb had started on his round of the jail. The prisoners were rummaging through their food tins to fish out something to present to their beloved leader. As we learnt later he accepted the gift from each prisoner and then put it in the prisoner's mouth, shook hands with him and moved on to the next prisoner. By and by he approached our barrack. A charismatic personality, he was accompanied by other leaders of the People's Party.

When he learnt that we were Indian prisoners he stopped in his tracks and intently surveyed us. "I feel hurt when I look at your plight," he said. "I can very well realise that the condition of Pakistani prisoners in Indian jails could not be any better than yours. But believe me, the day our Party comes into power, God willing, you will be sent back to your country within a year." When we heard this we could not help shouting, "Bhutto Saheb Zindabad!" He smiled and passed on waving to us.

This great man stood by his word. The Simla Agreement was a testimony to it. It was instituted within a year of his coming to power wherein it was clearly stated that along with the prisoners of war, the other civilian prisoners, whether smugglers, spies or hostages who had been arrested before the 1971 war would be exchanged between the two countries. I am sure that while making this agreement he had vividly in mind the promise he had made to us, Indian prisoners, in the Kot Lakhpat jail. Otherwise one had rarely heard of exchange of spies between two countries.

It was under the same agreement that our countrymen taken prisoners in 1953 were sent back to India along with us. The families of those Indians can never forget this great messiah who had a big hand in their repatriation.

Bhutto Saheb and his companions were lodged in the 'A' category first class barracks where the other Pakistani prisoners were not allowed to venture. It seemed the report of Bhutto

Saheb's meeting with the prisoners had reached the world outside. As a result strict security measures were enforced in the jail whereby Bhutto Sabeb could meet visitors only in the presence of the security police. But soon after that he was transferred to the Mianwali Jail and lodged in the Women's Section where later Sheikh Mujib also came to stay.

On the fifth day of our arrival in jail Samund Singh and I received a note on behalf of the Superintendent of the Jail that we were wanted in his office. The Superintendent showed me an order of the Governor of Punjab which read as follows:

The Governor of Punjab is pleased to order that Mohan Lal Bhaskar alias Mohammed Aslam should be put in solitary confinement for six months on the charge of illegal activities which have proved dangerous to the security of Pakistan.

This solitary confinement was imposed under Section 29 of the Defence of Pakistan Rules. A similar order was passed against Baba Samund Singh. We were immediately handed over to Chaudhri Manzur Hussain, Sub-Inspector Special Branch CID, Shahi Qila, Lahore. He was present in the jail office in mufti and had two constables with him. They blindfolded and handcuffed us after which we were driven off in a station wagon through the bazaars in the direction of Shahi Qila.

Shahi Qila, Lahore: Hell on Earth

After a slow climb the station wagon came to a halt. They helped me down the vehicle and led me up a flight of stairs. When they removed the bandage from my eyes I found myself standing in a big hall. Fear seemed to pervade the atmosphere as one generally experience in a suspense film. The place looked like an abode of ghosts. I could hear some sinister noises emanating from the far corners, mixed with men's screams as if they were slowly being butchered with a sharp knife. In these screams I heard a sing-song voice which I could easily recognise among a thousand voices. Thumping an empty pitcher, Khoh Singh was blithely singing to the tune of the famous Pakistani singer, Inayat-I-Hussain Bhatti.

I hold sway over Wagha border

Where lies a big maidan swarming with pimps.

I enjoy the game of killing pimps.

I go after the hand-picked ones,

Counting them one by one.

I was pleased to hear his voice. So he was still alive. That night when they had taken him away in a jeep from 596 FIU, Lahore I had felt that I was seeing the last of him; they might have at last decided to gun him down. But that happy-go-lucky Khoh Singh was still alive and somewhere quite close to me.

Chaudhri Manzur asked me to follow him, a man armed with a gun, walking a few steps behind me. They took me to an underground cellar and locked me up in a cell. Four blankets had been laid out for me. They also gave me tea in the evening. Here interrogation was done round the clock. This Center resembled our Amritsar Centre. Many Indian officers have been here for a long time. The CID Special Branch of shahi Qila had come into existence in 1965 and from then on the Shahi Qila had all along remained its headquarters with branches in all parts of Pakistan. Some of the sentries who later became friendly with me told me that ten Indian prisoners had died in the Qila in the course of interrogation and many more had gone mad.

Here the prisoners are kept in twelve separate cells, all at a distance from one another. The normal pattern is: one prisoner, one cell, one sentry. A sentry is changed every three hours and this sequence continues round the clock. An officer handles only one prisoner at a time and till his interrogation is complete he does not take on another. After the enquiry is over six officers take over that prisoner simultaneously and keep plying him with questions. A prisoner is not let off the hook until they are fully satisfied.

The Special Branch is located in the right part of the fort up a slope and is enclosed by an eight-foot high wall. The rest of the foil is open to the public to which a nominal entry fee is charged. It has an extensive green lawn where people come for picnics. The premises within the wall where the Special Branch is housed is out of bounds to the public. Only a little way off the Qila is located the Tibbi Bazaar, the notorious redlight district of Lahore where about six thousand prostitutes carry on their flesh trade. As the evening approaches revellers swarm to the place in large numbers. From cheap sluts to high class prostitutes whose rates range from one rupee to a thousand rupees a night, the latter doing their business on the sly in the guise of songstresses, are there for the entertainment of their customers. Many of them decked up in finery prowl round the lawns of the fort in daytime in search of customers. Imagine the existence of torture chambers so close to this place of revellery.

The Shahi Qila covers a huge area which can hold nothing short of five lakh people. An army used to be stationed here in the times of Maharaja Ranjit Singh. The construction of the fort was started during the times of Emperor Shahjahan and was completed in the times of Maharaja Ranjit Singh.

The Shahi Masjid, another important landmark, is not far

from the fort and right in front of the main gate of the fort there is Guru Arjun Dev's Gurudwara where he attained his martyrdom. It makes one's flesh creep when one visualises how the Guru must have sat there with closed eyes intoning *Wahe Guru, Wahe Guru* while his tormentors poured burning sand over his head. Now the Gurudwara is being renovated to enhance its appearance.

The underground cellar where I was lodged used to be an elephant stable during the times of Maharajas. The pachyderms used to massage their massive bodies against its four-foot thick pillars. The rays of the sun won't reach here. The only *munshi* (clerk) Bashir was the incharge of our cells. Given to tongue-lashing he would never address any one without a swear word.

One evening the lock on my door was opened and I was led upstairs. When they removed the bandage from my eyes, I found myself standing before Major Aijaz Maqsood. I salaamed him. He gestured me to take the chair and enquired about my health. After some inconsequential talk he got down to business. He said, "Bhaskar, if you agree to add to your statement that you had met Major Arif in Gulberg that night, then I can promise on oath that I'll release you and have you sent back to your country."

I thought over the matter for an instant and realised in a flash what was at the back of his mind – personal jealousy. Major Arif must be senior to him and probably was coming in the way of his promotion. Evidently, there was no love lost between the two and Major Maqsood wanted to fire the gun from my shoulder.

"Major Saheb, you know there is no truth in what you are saying," I replied. "In the statement that I have made earlier there is no mention of this. I don't want to invite trouble for myself by changing the statement at this stage."

"You need not worry about it," Major Maqsood assured me. "It's no problem for me to change your statement. Your statement is still with me. I can have it re-typed. All I need is your consent."

This handsome man suddenly fell from my esteem; he looked so replusive to me as if his fair complexion was marred by leprosy. He was trying to play dirty with one of his own brother officers. Could anything be meaner than that? The other man's only fault was that he was senior to Major Maqsood. At that time I was in a condition to give vent to my loathing for him.

"There's a good news for you," Major Maqsood said, trying to take advantage of my silence. "Your comrade Amrik Singh who had betrayed you and was instrumental in your arrest has himself been put under arrest. He is lodged in one of the cells here."

"This has served Amrik Singh right," I replied. Suddenly my mind ran over the pages of history which provided the parallel to it. Alauddin had handed down a similar reward to Raja Ambhi and Mohammed Ghori to Raja Jai Chand. Since history bore testimony to it, the treatment meted out to Amrik Singh caused me no surprise or happiness.

"I'm sorry, I'm unable to oblige you," I told Major Maqsood. "I've no enmity against Major Arif. I lack the guts to bear the curses of his family. God will never forgive me for this misdemeanour of mine. Even if you let me off, he will put me in someone else's clutches. His hands are long and far-reaching. Therefore, I crave your forgiveness. I'm sorry I'll not be into it."

"Don't be a fool," Major Maqsood growled. "It'll do you no good to be so adamant. Think of yourself. Think of your aged parents. And of your wife and of the child yet to be born."

So he was trying to play on my sentiments. "God is their protection. Where do I come into this picture?" I said. "I'm just an insignificant creature and am not prepared to commit such a sin. There are many other Indians whose cases are under your investigation. Why not ask one of them? He may be willing to oblige you. But please keep me out of it."

"It's not just a question of statement," he said. "Your word will carry weight. Of all the Indian spies caught so far you are the most educated."

"Forgive me, Major Saheb, I'm not prepared for it," I said with an air of finality.

His hand fell heavily on the table bell. "Throw him into

that dungeon," he shouted to the sentry, livid with rage. "This unfortunate wretch – it's not in his fate to be released."

I had a most peaceful sleep that night. Sometimes goodness is its own reward. A sinner has no peace of mind. He resorts to liquor and sleeping pills to fall asleep but his own mind becomes his worst enemy. Goodness, on the other hand works like perfume on one's mind. I was in one such happy frame of mind that night.

Raja Gul-Anar Khan: A Chandravanshi Rajput

Even the old walls of the Shahi Qila shook and the hearts of the inmates of the cells sank as he bellowed at someone. They would pray in a cringing voice, "Oh God, let Gul-Anar Khan not be assigned to investigate our case!" Most of the 'accused' when they came out of his room had twisted fingers, broken limbs or a limping gait. He was a terrorist - a living terror. DSP Sheikh Abdul Rahman, Chaudhri Afzal Beg alias Mohammed Azim Durrani and one Malik Saheb were known for their brutality. An old man known as Khan, who had cat's eyes was said to be adept in reading one's mind like an open book. But Raja Gul Anar, although a Sub-Inspector, left them all miles behind. He was held in the highest esteem by his superiors and had the last word in everything. He was a handsome young man of 28 and his mode of investigation was such that the victim automatically played like a gramophone record in his presence. If the victim faltered he would pounce upon him with the agility of a cheetah and the next moment the victim would find one of his limbs maimed. He was very dedicated to his job and extended his investigations far into the night.

One day as the birds started chirping I thought that the morning had arrived. I washed myself and sat down to pray. An hour later my door creaked and I saw Munshi Bashir standing in the door. He asked me to come out. As usual, I was handcuffed and a gunman followed me. A shiver ran down my spine. They must be taking me to a torture chamber. I completely lost my nerve when I was pushed into the presence of Raja Gul-Anar Khan who was known as the *jallad* (executioner) of the Shahi Qila. I was going to sit down on the ground when with a nod of his bead he indicated me to take a chair. Munshi Bashir had left but the sentry was still there. By a sign he asked him to remove my hand-cuffs and leave the room.

Then he said, "Tell me one thing. What's the meaning of Bhaskar? And what's your caste?"

"Janab, Bhaskar means the sun and I'm a Brahmin by caste."

"So you're a Suryavanshi Brahmin?"

I looked at him in surprise. "Janab, how do you know this word?"

"There's nothing to be surprised about it. I've graduated in history. For that matter I'm myself a Chandravanshi Rajput. My ancestors were Rajas back in Rajasthan. That was in the times of Aurangzeb who believed in oppressing the the Hindus – specially the Rajputs. My great great-grand-father who was the Raja of a small principality in Rajputana ran away from that place for dear life. His wife was pregnant at that time. His caravan was passing through the desert when she started having labour pains and she gave birth to my great-grand-father behind a green bush. Because of this green bush he came to be called Haria. Posing as Muslims, the people constituting the caravan reached Jhangsur, Sargodha and settled there. Even now we have palatial houses there.

"It so happened," he continued "that my great great grandfather was forced to accept Islam under duress and in consequence his brother excommunicated him from their fold. Had it happened in Rajputana I fear he would have even been deprived of his property. It being an alien country his brothers could not have their way in this regard. Do you know why Islam spread so rapidly in India and why the people of this region have such a great hatred for the Hindus? True, that they were themselves Hindus once upon a time – generation after generation in fact. But the Hindus themselves were their own undoing.

"When the Muslims invaded India, the Hindu Rajas of various states, turn by turn, sided with the invaders, they did this to spite their own kinsmen which in the end proved to be the cause of their own ruination. Another reason was that those Hindus who read the *kalma* and embraced Islam – just to keep up appearances – were spurned by the other Hindus and they refused to take them back into their fold. They broke all ties with them and went to the extent of confiscating their lands and properties. And the worst of it, they refused to communicate with them, much less eat with them. The upshot was that these people took refuge under Islam and turned rabid enemies of the Hindus.

"It is a deep-rooted enmity which manifests itself even today, perhaps more than before, making the two communities fly at each other's throats. An Arab Muslim will happily share food with an Indian at the same table, but not an Indian Muslim. He would even shy away from a Hindu's shadow.

"My late grand-father used to tell me that his great-grand-father had embraced Islam under very trying circumstances when he found himself forced against the wall. His brothers had turned their backs upon him and he and his children were debarred from entering the temple. They did not even invite them on such festive occasions as Holi and Diwali. On the contrary, they warned their children not to accept any eatable from my great-grand-father's children. My great-grand-father tried to make his brothers see reason, he even begged of them on bent knees but that cut no ice with these custodians of the Hindu religion. The Hindu *Banias* constructed more, and more temples and spent lavishly to embellish them while lakhs and lakhs of Hindus starved. This strengthened the roots of Islam in India.

"It was these derelict Hindus whom Islam hugged to its heart. When they looked back into their past they decided to wreak vengeance on these selfish and narrow-minded Hindus. Those who did not even touch meat started eating beef and made it a point to do all those things that were anathema to the Hindus and would hurt their feelings. How could they forget that once the Hindus themselves had treated them in similar manner and had rode rough shod over them? Now tell me who was at fault?" Raja Gul-Anar stopped for an answer.

"Of course, our ancestors were responsible for it," I replied. "And among them the Brahmins most of all, who could not take stock of the situation and thus failed to guide the people on the right path. Today their misdeeds have recoiled upon their children."

"But you are also a Brahmin, aren't you?"

"Yes, I'm. But not one of those spurious Brahmins. The house in a lane of Abohar where I was born had only one Hindu family living in that lane – that's mine. The rest were all Muslims. The mid-wife who assisted my mother in bringing me into this world was a Muslim woman by the name of Raiba. Mian Irfan was my childhood friend. At the time of the partition when he came to say good-bye to me I clung to him and said that I will not let him go. At that time my father was posted as a senior constable at the Abohar police station. With the departure of the senior Muslim police officers he was in a way, the de facto in-charge of the police station. He engaged a bus and safely escorted all the Muslims of our lane across the border under his own supervision. Even today,

Chaudhri Nisar Ahmed, Sub-Inspector of Naulakha police station will bear me out that my father was on the friendliest of terms with the Muslims. He counted Nisar Saheb among his friends. My case was under his investigation at the Naulakha police station. When he learnt that I was Pandit Amin Chand's son tears came to his eyes. In spite of physical remand he did not even touch me, nor did he allow anyone else to take liberties with me. He was very considerate to me."

"Don't speak about it to anyone else." Gul-Anar Khan warned me. "Our people are very suspicious. His goodness of heart can lead him to trouble. Of course, my case is different. Well, Bhaskar, you have been telling me that this man was very kind to you and that your plight even drew tears from his eyes. But why was he so kind to you in spite of your being the worst enemy of our nation?"

"Perhaps you don't understand," he added after a pause. "Well, let me explain. Even if you know the rudiments of psychology you will get a hang of the whole thing. Chaudhri Nisar Ahmed's manifestation of love for you is the result of his regard for Hinduism which has remained dormant in him for centuries. The feeling had sunk into his subconscious mind and due to the force of circumstances his ancestors never allowed it to come to the surface. You are just a pretext to become the conduit to express his dormant feelings and getting this outlet they broke all bounds like the bursting of a dam. In fact behind the facade of your father's friendship he was

68

unwittingly shedding tears over the Hindu religion which once upon a time his ancestors professed.

"A pity that your religion which had risen to great heights of philosophy and is based on compassion was annihilated by its own adherents. Even today it is gasping for breath because of the deficiency of its own followers. Even today if your religious leaders profess goodwill towards the Muslims of this region there is no reason why they should not again come closer. It's their own blood running through others' veins. There are many things in our own religion which rankle in our minds but we cannot speak against them. Our own illiterate mullahs and maulvis castigate us for it, branding us as *Kafirs*. For instance, our women have no right of equality. A man can marry four wives and divorce them any time at his sweet will. For this reason our women are having a miserable existence. With education there has been a slight improvement in their social status. Otherwise, as a student of history you would know that the Muslim kings maintained huge harems where women were lined up for their carnal pleasure.

"Even today in the Arabian countries their Amirs do not even know the names of their concubines; perhaps they would even fail to recognise some of them. If an uncle dies it's the nephew's inherent right to marry his so-called aunts if he so desires. It's a common practice for uncle's sons to seduce their own cousins.

"I'll tell you a lewd joke. Two cousins were travelling from

Karachi to Lahore. It was winter and their coupe was reserved. Their own sisters were also travelling with them. One cousin said to the other, "Mian, it's very cold. Can you suggest some way of keeping ourselves warm?" "Easy," replied the other. "You sleep with my sister and I will sleep with your's." Running feuds between families on account of such clandestine relations are not uncommon. It even ends in bloodshed. As a result the whole nation is sex starved which is leading it towards destruction.

"We abide by only those tenets of the Holy Quran which suit us and ignore others under the facade of modernism which are likely to cause us financial loss. According to the *Sharha* usury is a sin. One should neither give nor take loans for the sake of interest. But in actual practice things are just the other way round. Those who follow the tenets of the Quran are leading a miserable life while the usurers are having a whale of a time. This world itself is like a Paradise to them.

"My Allah, if my countrymen were to hear me uttering this blasphemy they would hang me or stone me to death. They are such terrible fanatics in Pakistan. What to talk of the illiterates, even the educated here scoff at rational thinking. The mullah have such stranglehold over us that we cannot budge an inch from where we are asked to stand. We cannot contemplate any change in our religion, although according to the present times, it requires radical changes. We also require a Martin Luther to bring about reforms in out religion." He suddenly fell silent.

"What do you think of secularism?" I could not help asking him.

"A wonderful thing!" he beamed. "Perhaps that's what has saved democracy from getting extinct in India. There a dictator can never find a foot-hold. People would refuse to toe the line on the basis of religion. But in Pakistan anyone who wields power can become a dictator. It makes no difference whether it is Ayub or someone else. He has only to declare that he is the saviour of Islam. In Pakistan, if we also had the Hindus and Sikhs to hold the political balance, I can assure you that we too would have been breathing freely in a democratic set-up." He rang the bell and asked the peon to send in my food.

"Bhaskar, have your food and we can continue with our talk after you have finished your food." He went out and bolted the door from outside.

While eating I reflected over the whole matter. Our ancestors had indeed behaved in a mean manner, putting Kabir's and Guru Nanak's teachings at naught. Even during our own time, although Gandhi sacrificed his life we still continue to follow the path which creates strife and discord between two faiths. Even our ruling princes induced their people to follow the path of hatred. They kept people in water-tight compartments in the name of caste.

If a Brahmin's job is to sow the seeds of discord in the name of caste I am ashamed that I was born among them. The brains of our ancestors must have remained empty of all wisdom that they danced as puppets to the tune of the Brahmins. When Lord krishna himself did not believe in such shibboleths, Lord Ram could accept wild plums from the hands of a low-born Bhilni Shabri, then what rationale have the Brahmins to ran such irrational thoughts into our heads? I have come to the conclusion that the Brahmins had sold themselves to the Rajas for their own gains and danced to their whims. They divided the entire nation into factions so that the Rajas could tyrranise over the people untrammeled, and hold on to the seat of power. In the end, after an oppression lasting over centuries these people rose in revolt against their rulers. Our ancestors had indeed been extremely foolish. They had forced the menials live outside the city limits and had tied bells round their necks to warn the high caste Hindus lest the shadow of these menials should pollute them.

My chain of thoughts broke as Raja Gul-Anar Khan entered the room.

"Well, Bhaskar what's this story about the Atomic Energy Commission?" he abruptly asked. "The high-ups are eager to know about it and are pressing us to find out."

His question angered me. "It's all a concoction of that lover of his sister," I replied.

"Who's this lover of his sister? Where does be live?"

I suddenly realised my mistake. I should not have pointed in the direction where Amrik Singh was lodged. "I mean Amrik

Singh," I said. "I wish I knew where he is now."

"Don't try to make a fool of me, Bhaskar. You know very well where he is now. Now out with the truth. Don't you know where he is now?" he asked in a threatening voice. So he was showing his nailed fig. I realised it was futile to hide things from him. "Raja Sabeb, I know he's somewhere in this very fort."

His face turned red with rage, making me shake with fear.

"So you are trying to rope in our own men?" he said. "I say name that son of pimp who had given you that secret."

"Raja Saheb, he's none of your sentries, not any man is this fort. He is Major Maqsood of 596 FIU, Lahore, who had met me a few days back and told me in passing that Amrik Singh was lodged in this fort. Please believe me, no one else has talked to me about it."

He was surprised at my boldness. He immediately dialled FIU and got in touch with Major Maqsood. After satisfying himself, he banged the receiver and turned to me. "You're saved, Bhaskar," he growled. "Otherwise hell would have been let loose upon you. If any of our sentries had talked about it I would have cashiered him on the spot and hung both of you upside down. "what else did that *haramzada* ask you?"

"Nothing else," I replied nonchalantly I wanted to tell him about Major Maqsood's evil designs against his fellow officer but desisted. Raja, however sensed that there was something up my sleeve. "Don't hide anything from me," he said. "I know you were with him for full one hour."

I disgorged everything about Major Maqsood.

Raja's face changed colour and he fumed at the Major hurling the choicest abuses at him in absentia. "I'll see how that *haramzada* dares enter this fort. I'll have him chucked out from the FIU also. What an intriguing fellow, indeed! Today every place is swarming with such paper tigers. They eat dirt but dream of climbing up the ladder even if they have to adopt questionable means to achieve their ends. I'll write to the Army Head Quarters so that this well-meaning officer does not become the victim of this fellow's abominable moves."

"Raja Saheb, now the cat is out of the bag. I know that Amrik Singh has been arrested. Will you be good enough to tell me what's the charge against him? He was a very useful man to you."

"A traitor does not command respect anywhere. I've more regard for you than for that pimp. Your entire gang has been apprehended and we have no more need for him. Why should we keep him in our pay? And if we do not pay him he can turn against us and do us harm. So the best place for him is behind the bars."

"How long are you going to keep him interned?"

"At least for fifteen years."

"And what about me?"

"Your fate is just the same as his. Neither better nor worse."

"I hear you are going to kill me."

"No, we'll throw you in some dungeon to die your own death there."

"Is there no chance of my being repatriated?"

"No, none that I can think of. The people who were caught fifteen years ago are still rotting in jail. If by mistake they happen to look at their faces in the mirror they would not be able to recognise themselves. Well, you are asking too many questions. More than are good for you. Here, take this pen and paper and write down your statement. Don't let gloom weigh on your mind. Mysterious are the ways of Allah. You never know when the tide turns in your favour and washes you ashore. But for Allah's sake don't hold back anything. Put down everything in black and white. I don't want to be hard on you. If once the round of torture starts there will be no end to it. Try to save yourself against such an ugly possibility. We shall again meet the day after."

He rang the bell. The sentry came in and after blind-folding me led me back to my cell.

My first day of investigation did not go off badly. I took my food and went to sleep, lost in thoughts. Will he throughout treat me in this manner? Then I recalled the moment when his mood had suddenly changed and he had glared at me. How long could the Hindu blood coursing through his veins protect me? Would not his Muslim hatred for the Hindus assert itself? I slid into sleep lost in these thoughts.

It had taken me two days to prepare my statement. On the third day I was again led into the investigation room. Raja Gul-Anar Khan was there.

"Asalam-ulekam!" I said. "Namaskar!" Raja Saheb replied, a faint smile playing across his face.

I placed my statement before him and he started reading it. Perhaps he had already gone through my 596 FIU statement. His mouth fell open. "Ya Khuda!" be exclaimed. "Bhaskar, you're a wonderful man.

"Why, Janab, What's happened?"

"You've a photographic memory. There is not even a change of comma between your earlier and this statement. One would think that someone had dictated you the earlier statement and you had transcribed it on this sheet of paper. Now I'm convinced that there is no truth in that Atomic Energy Commission story. If you have anything else to say let me hear it now."

"No, Janab, I've nothing more to say."

"Then that settles it. I'll get your statement typed and send it to the higher authorities. If they are satisfied a case will be instituted against you. Otherwise, you will again be called for further interrogation, till then I'll call you every day. Come, let's sit in the sun. It's very chilly here. We shall have a chat. That will divert my mind. You see, I've to deal with junglees like you and that has also made me a brute. You people are so hard on yourselves. You just lift your faces without a thought

76

and walk into Pakistan as if it belongs to your father-in-law and a red-carpet welcome is awaiting you here. That's what makes me so angry. The heartless manner in which you had treated my forebears still haunts me. And then I lose my head. They treated us like animals. I go one better and treat you people like dogs. I don't know why I talk to you so nicely. The day you came here I studied your case history and felt that Allah had already punished you more than you deserve. He has deprived you of your sweet home and an equally sweet wife whom you had married only a short time ago. As I note she was pregnant at the time you were caught. I feel sorry for you. Just look in that direction."

We were sitting on the roof overlooking the lawn of the Shahi Qila where hundreds of men, women and children were strolling around, a good many of them couples. Only a few women were in burqua. The rest of them were in salwar-kamiz or saris. Sitting on the roof I felt as if I was the Mughal emperor Akbar watching below the Meena Bazaar of Delhi. Lured by my imagination I saw no difference in the gay crowd below and that bazaar of yore.

"Bhaskar, enjoy yourself as long as you are with me. After that it's anybody's guess what you'll be in for. Ya Khuda, I've seen the plight of the Indian prisoners in the Kot Lakhpat Jail. It sent a tremor through my heart. Bad food, dirty clothes, many of them gone insane and throwing stones at one another. There were still others who ran amuck and had to be kept

77

apart from others. There were still others who prayed for death. You are lucky that you don't smoke. I have seen prisoners standing near the gate and begging for half-smoked cigarettes."

"I have heard about them but I've not seen them," I said. "I was kept in the death cell from where I was directly brought here. The Indians I happened to see seemed to be all right. The Pakistani prisoners, particularly those who had been awarded capital punishment were extraordinarily nice to the Indians. They hoped that because of their kindness God may relent at the last moment and they may be saved from the gallows."

"One thing that keeps them from going off the rails is that they are under-trials," Raja Gul-Anar said. "They are therefore not subjected to hard labour. Otherwise, Pakistani jails are like hell for the Indians. You just wait, you'll see for yourself."

"Raja Saheb, who knows what kind of fate awaits me. The Benefactor who has shielded me so far may yet give me a better deal and I may go back home."

"I wish it could come true. But it is like hoping against hope. If your hope is not realised you may get a serious jolt which you may not be able to stand and may lose your balance of mind like so many of them. Oh, hell, leave these thoughts alone! Let us talk of something more pleasant. Yes, let's talk about your religion which once also happened to be our religion. Why do you Brahmins dupe simpletons?"

"Raja Saheb, this is a long story relating to the time which saw our community steadily going downhill. You may not be knowing anything about it. I am talking of long long ago – of a period which we Hindus called the *Sat Yuga*. People had enough to eat and they considered it their greatest duty to meditate and pray which was supposed to bring them salvation. Do you have another example of Rama in the history of man ? Or another Buddha or Ashoka?

"I'm talking of the times when people of our country sought out and honoured our learned men, philosophers and scientists and begged to guide them the path of enlightenment. They were the men who possessed the ultimate knowledge and knew about Brahma, the creater of the universe. That was why they were given the appelation of Brahmins, their main object in life being to enlighten the people. They led a dedicated life, doing nothing else but that. In our country education ingrained in one tolerance and taught one to live a life of self-denial. People on their part considered it their duty to compliment the basic needs of the Brahmins.

"But as time passed their decline set in. Lord Krishna mentioned in the Gita the advent of the *Kaliyuga* – the dark ages in the cyclical evolution of time. People started denigrating the Brahmins, bringing them down from their exalted pedestal, forcing them to think of ways to keep their bodies and souls together. They started hoodwinking people in the names of myriad gods constituting the Indian pantheon to which the ignorant and superstitious people fell an easy prey. If you read the Gita you will know that by *Kaliyuga*, Lord Krishna implies the machine age. It is also said that *Kaliyuga* will be the age of strife and discord."

"Bhaskar, there's truth in every word that you have said," said Raja. "Discord is sampant wherever you look – in the village, in the lane and in home. For that matter it takes the entire country in its sweep. People are hungry and poverty will not let them out of its grip. Lord Krishna, as you have explained, has gone to the heart of the truth. I feel like genuflecting to him right now. The nation that did not pay heed to his warning could not have but sunk to the depths of mental degeneration."

"Taxila, which is now in Pakistan used to be the leading university of the Hindus," I reminded Raja Sabeb. "But it is a sad state of affairs that now the youths of our country look to other countries for higher education."

"Our country too is no better in this regard," Raja Saheb rejoined. "If anything, it is worse. We look down upon the intellectual elite of our own country and blindly pander to the intellectuals of other countries. Ours is a filthy country. Not fit to live in. The very foundations of our old religion have been shaken. There is no peace of mind. Like hungry dogs we hanker after wine, women and wealth." Raja Sabeb suddenly became thoughtful.

"Raja Saheb, I could not agree with you more," I said "Every right thinking person of this great sub-continent, which covers India and Pakistan holds similar views. But the world around us is such that we are reduced to being mere puppets. In a way, we are no better than small children who amuse themselves by running about blowing bubbles. If you think of it, our life is nothing but a rat race and in the end when the naked truth mocks at us we find it's too late to mend ourselves. We are like those ruins which crumble down noiselessly. No weight is required to sink a man fallen in a well; he will go down by his own weight. Mankind is so heavily weighed down by the load of its own sins that it has already started sinking."

"How beautifully you talk, Bhaskar. Are you a poet by any chance?"

"A poet only in name," I replied "But I've had the good fortune of being close to the Hindi poet Bacchan. I have also had the good luck of listening to Nazir Banarasi, Mela Ram Wafa and Ata Mohammed from very close quarters. Perhaps that is why sometimes I begin to talk in the poetic vein. I have read the whole of Mirza Ghalib, Hakim Momin, Mir Taqui Mir, Sauda, Hafiz Jalandhari, Faiz Ahmed Faiz and Shakeel Badayuni. I myself write poetry in Hindi and some of my Hindi songs were recorded by the Star Hindi Recording Company when I was only eighteen years old. My pen-name is Madbu Mohan Bhaskar."

"What is Madhu?" he asked.

"She was my first love. The first of my adolescent loves. I was mad after her. I had first met her in Mussoorie. She was a student of Francis Girls Higher Secondary School, Daryaganj, New Delhi. Like the heroine of John Keats' poem, The Night, she bestowed tier love on me and then disappeared by giving me a wrong address. For months I wandered in the streets and lanes of Daryaganj in search of her. I even neglected my studies, so gone was I on her. This was in 1960 when the Hippies were unknown. But like the Hippies of the future I grew my hair long and in this I was almost ten years ahead of them. As I passed through streets boys and girls would laugh at me and make cat calls. But I did not care. I could think of nothing else but her. The result was that I failed in my Intermediate in Physics. It came as a great shock to me for I was considered to be a very bright student in the Matric I had scored 72 per cent marks. That brought me to my senses. I passed my exam. In September, the same year. And then I did B.A. as a private candidate and followed it up with a B.Ed. doing it from Moga. That's where I met my prospective wife. She acted as a balm in heating my scars."

"Where did you meet this *dalla* (pimp) of yours – I mean Amrik Singh?"

"I think my office people had blundered in putting me in touch with him. Later on spending a night with this bloke in the same room was perhaps a graver mistake."

"Bhaskar, I've spent an interesting day with you and I hope we shall have occasions to spend many more such days together. I've sympathy for you. Keep up your spirits. This is the only way one can remain cheerful. Sing songs and read books. We have a good library here. I'll have some books sent to you.

That will divert your mind."

After a short while Raja Saheb personally brought me two books in my cell - *The Riddles of the Universe and Lady Chatterley's Lover.* I had already read D.H. Lawrence's book and returned it to him, retaining the other one to read. It was an excellent book on the various religions of the world and opened up new vistas before my mind. I read it over and in the course of my reading I happened to meet Raja saheb many times. During my six months' stay in the fort I remained immune from any harassment. No one even slapped me.

On Ist March, 1969 Raja Saheb came to me early in the morning "Congratulations, Bhaskar!" he said. "You have become the father of a son."

"Janab, who has given you this information?"

"Our own man, who had been to Ferozpur. He brought me information. Don't you believe it?"

"Janab, there's no question of not believing you. But your poor enemy has no means of regaling you on this occasion. I've no sweets to offer."

"But I've brought the sweets. Here, have them. You must celebrate, the birth of my nephew."

I was deeply moved; it brought tears to my eyes.

He patted me on my back. "Be brave. Don't cry. He may prove lucky for you. You may go back home."

Although he was trying to console me I saw tears in his own

eyes. He left abruptly. I am not capable of describing my condition at that time.

The days dragged on – one day and then another. Sometimes I thought of my parents , wife, child and others. What did my child look like? What will they tell him when he asked about his father? May be by the time I joined him he would be able to lisp. But what if it-did not happen that way? My heart would start sinking.

On 13th March Raja Saheb told me that I would soon be transferred to FIC Rawalpindi where I would be subjected to an intensive interrogation by senior officers.

The fateful day arrived. An Assistant Sub-Inspector along with two men came to fetch me. Raja Saheb shook my hand in farewell. There were tears in my eyes, as if I was going away leaving my heart behind. I was parting with a dear friend who had treated me like a precious guest in this slaughter house. I was handcuffed only in one hand and not blindfolded. After seven months I was again – seeing the bazaar of Lahore. But due to the martial law this time they looked so drab and colourless.

FIC: Rawalpindi

On the way the Assistant Sub-Inspector warned me: "Look, you'll not talk to anybody nor give any indication that you're a Hindustani. I've not blindfolded you so that you should not draw unnecessary attention. Our people are madcaps and they can be upto any mischief, making it difficult for us to control the situation. The effect of the t965 war is still lingering in their minds. If someone enquires I'll tell him that you are a Pakistani army deserter being taken back to your unit at Rawalpindi. You must corroborate my statement."

When we entered the rail compartment I was feeling very low. The train was about to start when Subedar Mohammed Aslam of the 596 FIU, Lahore suddenly barged into our compartment. He was furious when be saw that my eyes were not bandaged and only one hand of mine chained. He went hammer and tongs at the ASI. "Why haven't you tied his hands at his back?" he demanded to know. "And why no bandage on his eyes?" The ASI replied, "We shall be travelling at night in a closed compartment and I've two constables with me. Besides,

I don't want to make a show-piece of him before the public. If the people come to know who he is they can even manhandle him which will land me in real trouble."

"If you can't deal with trouble what are you carrying these arms for?" the Subedar countered. "Do as I tell you."

People had already collected outside our compartment and were shouting "Ya Ali!" The army jawans patrolling on the railway platform rushed up and drove away the crowd. Realising his folly, the Subedar quietly slipped away. The doors of my compartment were closed. The ASI removed the bandage from my eyes and again freed one of my hands. "These army people are devoid of brains," he grumbled. "They invite trouble with open arms. Now that *sala* Subedar has slunked off, leaving me to face the music. The irony of it, we have to obey this pack of fools, these sons of owls, because of the martial law."

When the train stopped at the next station many hands were furiously banging on our doors. Pakistanis had collected outside our compartment in their keenness to have a good look at me. The banging on the door became more frantic and we feared that the door may come off its hinges. The people were cursing the ASI for denying them the fun. It was a small wayside station where no military was in evidence. The situation seemed to be taking an ugly turn. The ASI once again cursed the Subedar who had created this headache for him. The mob started pelting stones on the compartment. It would be the height of folly to open the door at this juncture when the mob fury was at its worst.

Suddenly we heard machine gun fire and people running away screaming for life. Soon the platform became quiet. The ASI opened the door of the compartment and let up the window shutters. The Platoon Commander of a unit came to us and said, "The station master had telephoned me. You need not have any fear. We have taught those fellows a lesson. Four of them were injured. We have packed them off to the hospital. But how did these people come to know that you are escorting a Hindustani? You should have been more careful."

The angerged ASI laid the blame at the Subedar's door. The Platoon Commander stepped closer to me. "You bloody *kaflrs* are always creating trouble for us!" he shouted at me, giving a blow on my mouth.

"No, mister," the ASI cried from where he was standing. "You can't do that to him. Please move away from here. You can't touch him. It's my responsibility to protect him and escort him safely to his destination. That's what I'm here for" The Platoon Commander got out of the compartment muttering. The ASI instructed his constables to get down at every station and shoot down anyone who tried to create trouble.

"I'm sorry," he said, as he saw me pressing my cheek. "Don't worry, this will not happen again."

With the blow, one of my upper teeth had started aching and my head also seemed to be bursting with pain.

"What's the matter?" the ASI asked. "Something gone wrong?"

"Janab, I'm having an awful pain in my tooth."

"I'll get you some hot tea at the next station."

"Thank you, Janab."

It was an excruciating pain and I could not suppress my groans. Only those who have experienced it know how troublesome a toothache can be. A constable had a packet of cigarettes. I requested him to light a cigarette and give it to me. I touched my aching tooth with its burning end. It gave me slight relief. I repeated the treatment at reasonable intervals through the entire journey.

The incident reminded me of our neighbour Nathu washerman, who used to treat my toothache in my childhood with hot compresses. I felt that the treatment in the modified form was doing me some good. At the next station a constable brought hot tea for me but the tea gave me no relief. It was now midnight and the train was scheduled to reach Rawalpindi at two. Would anybody take notice of my trouble there? Had I been in the Shahi Qila Raja Saheb would have promptly sent for a dentist. No doubt, the ASI was kind to me but he had his limitations. When one is in trouble the hours seem to become longer. The hands of the watch seemed to be moving with excruciating slowness. My two hours passed like two years.

The train at last reached Pindi. The ASI had to take me to

the cantomnent and locate the FIC which was quite a job for a stranger in that dark night. So he decided to lock me up in some police station and set out on his quest in the morning. While locking me up he casually mentioned to the Thana Inspector about my trouble. There was another Pathan in the lock-up. "Oe, Ahmede, give this man some opium," the Thana Inspector told the Pathan. The man got up groggily. His hand went up somewhere under his armpit and he produced a small opium pill for me.

"Not such a big pill!" the Inspector cried. "It'll kill him. Give him just a quarter of it. In the meanwhile I'll get him some tea."

I was taking opium for the first time. I thought it was something abominable. But now I realised that even bad things can be put to some good use. The pill acted like magic. I soon dozed off.

Early next morning we set out for the cantonment in a tonga. When the tonga reached the military hospital, I reminded the ASI to blindfold me and put handcuffs on my wrists. I knew that FIC was somewhere in the vicinity of the hospital. It was perhaps a Sunday or some holiday. The office was closed and only one havaldar, Abdul Rahman Khatak was on duty. Word was sent to Subedar Sher Khan about our arrival. A burly and happy-go-lucky type of man, he commended the ASI for bringing me handcuffed and blindfolded for he considered me to be a dangerous type of a Hindustani spy. He gave the ASI an official receipt in token of having taken charge of me from him as if I was a commodity. Unbandaged I found myself in a closed cell. It was here that I spent the next one and a quarter years of my jail life. Before leaving, the ASI had told them about my toothache. The Subedar sent for a phial of pheropyrene which proved quite effective. My toothache vanished with one application.

The office of FIC was located in a big building fenced by barbed wire. In those days there was a guard of one to eight, which meant that there were eight men under each commander. There were two men keeping watch over me round the clock. One would stand by me, holding a bayonet, while the other would go round the building. After completing the round he would take the place of the stationary guard who would in turn, go out on his round. This sequence would continue round the clock. On the following morning a new havaldar and his men would replace the earlier unit. This was done to guard against the possibility of the prisoner becoming friendly with any of the men of the guard.

The FIC was headed by a swollen-headed, ill-tempered Pathan named Major Kamal Raza Jadun. Another officer on the staff, Capt. Syyed, who had been trained in China was considered to be a torture-expert. There were two JCOs on the staff, Subedar Sher Khan and Naik Subedar Anwar. Among the clerks I knew one N.C.O. There was also Havaldar Abdul Rahman Khatak, a jovial sort, who was perhaps the only merciful man among brutes. I used to eat with the guards and was served the same kind of food which they ate.

I don't know why I had completely lost my appetite and an unknown fear had gripped me. I felt restless as if some invisible hands were advancing towards me. Sometimes I felt that like the Duchess of Malfi. I was surrounded by mad men who kept howling like jackals. Every morning a packet of K2 cigarettes was thrown into my cell which I refused to touch. Subedar Sher Khan asked me which brand of cigarettes I smoked. Since the cigarettes would be supplied from my regulation quota of rations, he said that he would have no problem in meeting my demand.

I did not smoke. But just out of fun, I told him that Three Castles was my favourite brand. I never thought that they would comply with my wishes. Three Castles was an expensive cigarette and in those days a packet cost no less than eight rupees. But to my utter surprise from the next day they started supplying me Three Castles cigarettes. This put me in a quandary: What should I do with these cigarettes? If I did not smoke them I would be taken for a liar, and if I smoked I would find it extremely distasteful. I hated cigarette smoke and my father was careful not to enter my room with a lighted cigarette. Now I started smoking like a habitual smoker and within a couple of days acquired a taste for cigarettes. After finishing my own quota I would beg the guard for cigarette stubs. He would throw a stub before me as one throwing a crumb before a dog.

In cigarettes I had discovered a genial companion for my loneliness. It may not be a good habit but it was an agreeable way of getting over my solitude. It was nice to fill my lonely hours with smoke. It appeared as if someone had blown away all my dreams with an explosive and their smoke was now hanging in the air. I breathed in that air.

It was my third day in this place. I heard the guard saluting someone. Then the door opened and I saw a stately, curly-haired Pathan officer entering my cell. He stopped and stared at me. I salaamed him. He acknowledged my salaam with a faint nod of his head and asked me how long I had stayed in the Shahi Qila.

"For about six months," I replied.

"What kind of tortures were you subjected to?"

"None, Janab, they did not even slap me."

"Hm!" His eyelids, fluttered. "Don't expect any such thing from us. You must come out with all the facts. Otherwise, we know how to make you disgorge them."

"I have told everything from the very beginning. That was why those officers at the Shahi Qila left me alone. I'm not their relative."

"Relatives my foot! You have not come out even with one per cent of the facts, not to talk of the whole truth. Don't try to be smart with us. I know you are an educated spy. But remember, one can't fool everybody. If you don't bother us we will not bother you. Otherwise, you know we can make your life hell for you. Don't forget, this is FIC– Final Interrogation Center of Pakistan. Here either a man goes to pieces or his breath gets snuffed out." He gave me a cunning smile and abruptly walked out, banging the door shut behind him.

My suspicion had come true. What I had feared most was now going to happen. An impending danger had already cast its shadow in advance. It was assuming fearsome shapes. This Final Interrogation Center could as well be the final stage of my life.

That evening when the food came I could not eat more than two morsels of it. It proved a boon in disguise. Soon Subedar Sher Khan came and ordered me to remove all my clothes except my underwear. Then he ordered me to roll up all the four blankets and place them on my head. I was ordered to keep walking all night. He handcuffed my one hand and instructed the guard commander that if I ever stopped walking he should drag me upto the railing and slap me. After every hour I was allowed to rest for five minutes.

Torture is torture and it knows no limit. If one is hell bent upon torturing someone one can devise a hundred and one ways of doing so. The Subedar had thought of that way for me that night. Having eaten little in the evening I was not feeling sleepy but the cold wind kept piercing through my body. I was greatly scared and the pain inflicted on me at FIU had also revived. I fell down unconscious at about three in the morning. The guard commander dragged me near the railing and slapped me. But I was insensible to all that. Then he splashed water over my face but even that failed to revive me. He sent a man to fetch the Subedar who used to keep with him the key to my hand-cuff. He came, broke the seal of the lock and opened it He felt my pulse. I was still breathing. He ordered my body to be rolled up in the blankets and dumped in a corner of my cell.

I came after about three hours and heard a sparrow chirping. It had its nest under the ceiling of my cell. The mullah was giving the call for the morning namaz. I rubbed my eyes. The sentry told me not to from my place and to lay still. I again covered myself with a blanket and soon fell asleep. When the Subedar came at eight I was awake and salaamed him. He responded to my salaam with an imperceptible nod of his head. They brought me the breakfast. I took nothing except a cup of tea. "How are you feeling?" he asked me. "Janab, I'm feeling terribly tired." "It's all your doing," he replied. "You must satisfy the Major Sabeb. That's the only way that you can save your skin. Otherwise, I no hope for you."

He went away and my cell was again locked up. My ears were attuned to the outside world. The vehicular traffic had increased. Cars and jeeps were coming and going. I wondered what could be the reason for this unusual activity. And soon I got the answer to my question. The door of my cell opened. I was blindfolded and handcuffed again and let out towards, what I guessed, was the torture chamber. When they removed the bandage from my eyes I saw Major Jadun, along with his full retinue. Dr. Syyed, a torture expert, was sitting by his side. A lot of bottles and injectibles were lying in a tray in front of him. It appeared as if they were going to have a big show.

Dr. Syyed made me sit down by his side and turning my eyelids, poured some thick solution in my eyes after which he handed me a newspaper and asked me to read. I could not make out anything on the page. Everything looked so hazy and bluffed. Perhaps he wanted to create the scare in my mind that my eyesight had been damaged. But I knew it was all acting. I wanted to wipe my eyes but my hands were tied behind my back. To impress upon me that there was nothing false about what they were doing, Dr Syyed whispered something in the Major's ear and then said in a loud voice, "All right I'll have pity on the fellow and restore his eyesight. He picked up a syringe and gave a shot in my arm. Then he untied my hands and asked me to wipe my eyes. After wiping my eyes I found that my vision had cleared; there was nothing hazy about it.

I said, "Captain Sabeb, why are you harassing me and putting yourself to unneccessary trouble? This injection of morphia is not going to act on me. I can down a full bottle of whisky and yet walk steadily. This *tamasha* is not going to dupe me. I know you want to demoralise me. If your victim knows your

95

design your effort is bound to prove infructuous. You had poured gum in my eyes to create the impression that I was losing my vision."

He screwed his eyes in anger. "Oh, I didn't know that you are a drunkard," he fumed. *"Sala !* But I know how to deal with the likes of you." He gave me one more injection of morphia which suddenly increased my blood pressure and after a few minutes I started losing my consciousness. Now he got on to the real job of probing my mind. Acting on my sub-conscious mind he suggested that I had once mentioned a particular name. "It's made of how many letters?" I asked. "Five letters," he replied. On hearing him, I reeled out five names, one after the other: Hamid, Salim, Rafiq, etc. The tape-recorder was on. My hands were tied to a rope hanging from the ceiling. Whatever I mumbled was being duly recorded though I was not aware of what I was saying. However, it transpired that I had not said anything incriminating. Before coming here I had repeated my concocted story so often that it had left an imprint on my sub-conscious mind, rendering their psychological devices futile.

I regained my normal consciousness after twenty-six hours though I was still feeling a bit dazed. I was still in the same room and Dr. Syyed was standing before me, smiling. "Bhaskar, you have at last shown us the way," he said. "You have given us the names of all those Atomic Energy Commission chaps. You'll have the list of those names in a short while."

"Your glory will be short-lived," I said nonchalantly for by now I was past caring. "It will lead you nowhere. You'll only be harassing some innocent people for nothing."

"Don't try to put me off the track. I know you have friends whom you want to save."

I saw a car stopping inside the boundary wall. Two men from the office clad in mufti got down from the car followed by two smartly dressed sophisticated looking strangers. From their bearings they did not seem to fit into this place. Poor fellows, little did they know that they were walking into a trap. They were like innocent lambs being pushed towards wolves who were eagerly waiting to tear them apart.

"Do you recognise this man?" The two men in dress suits were asked.

The two men looked at me, puzzled. "We don't understand what's going on here," one of them said. "We were told that Dr. Figar wanted to have a discussion with us on heavy water."

Major Jadtin gave a satanic laugh. "You're right," he said. "It's precisely about that heavy water file which you sold this man for Rs. 13,000 and about your friend in the Security Section of the Commission who rendered you full assistance."

Their faces suddenly turned pale. I was immediately removed from there. But I kept hearing the screams of these two people for two hours. They were pleading innocence but no one was prepared to believe them. Still crying they were shoved into the cells situated on the right and left of my own cell. But I could not talk with them. Before leaving his office the Subedar came to me. "Now what have you to say, son?" he asked me. "You are being cruel to innocent people – that's all I can say," I replied. "Of course, you're right," he gave me a sarcastic smile. "They am as innocent as you. You just wait. We shall soon have a heart to heart talk. Even your bones will not find their way back to your country. You just wait and see, as I've told you." He walked out and slammed the door to shut.

For six months they kept beating those two people and me also into the bargain. I will describe later how these two were relieved from the clutches of their tormentors. And also how they stopped harassing me. This I will do in the context of my meeting with General Gul Hasan. Before I do so I must say something about Major Kamal Raza Jadun, Subedar Sher Khan and the kind-hearted Abdul Rahman Khatak.

Major Kamal Raza Jadun

M ajor Kamal Raza Jadun was as big a fool as he was heartless. His behaviour reminded me of those naughty children who while returning from school pelt stones at caged circus lions and then jeer at them. The Major would suddenly open my cell door and give me a cunning smile, akin to the one seen on the face of a prostitute's pimp. "Tell me, Maharaj," he would leer at me, "are you praying for your salvation? A pity that the doors of salvation are closed upon you, because you have out of your own sweet will got yourself circumcised and turned a Muslim. But don't worry, we shall soon arrange, for your passage to Heaven." Like foolish children he would make faces at me and then guffaw like the Ravana at the Ramlila. "Bhaskar, dear boy, I'll see to it that you're fixed here right and proper for the next twenty years,"

He would often come to his office dead drunk at night and give foolish instructions to the guards. The Subedar who was acquainted with his queer ways avoided showing up at night. One night the Major came dead drunk to has office and ordered his guard commander to bring him a prostitute from the nearby red-light district. The guard commander reported the matter to the Subedar. "Don't take any notice of him," the Subedar advised him. "Let him keep blubbering. He will go away after sometime. You stay on till the change of the guards at eight."

The whole night the FIC office kept resounding with the Major's cries and abuses. When he regained his senses he quietly walked away and was not seen for the next couple of days. Perhaps he had gone on leave to get over his discomfiture.

When he returned they told him that I was spitting blood with sputum. He ordered the Subedar to arrange for my X-ray at the Military Hospital at Rawalpindi.

I was taken to the hospital in a station wagon and the X-ray report which came after three days revealed that there was nothing wrong with me. But then what could account for the blood in my sputum? Could it be the first indication of TB? But the stupid Major seemed to be after my life. He would devise ingenious ways of torturing me. Sometimes he would order that I should eat the food and drink tea like animals, lapping the things up with tongue, without in any way using my hands. If I refused they would beat me till I complied with their wishes. He would swear that he would not relent till he had reduced me to the level of a pig.

His vagaries increased as time passed taking a heavy toll on my patience. I thought that since these people were determined to kill me why shouldn't I rebel against them which in any case would bring my end nearer. I tore off my clothes and would remain naked. I also stopped shaving. I ate only once a day. In three months my beard grew quite long and the hair on my head fell over my shoulders. For lack of cleanliness my hair was infested with lice. One night the Major ordered that each hair of my beard should be plucked out singly in the morning. Just to find out how painful the process could be I tried my hand at plucking my hair. I was at it the whole night. I realised that it is not so painful when one does it oneself. By morning my beard and moustache were devoid of any hair.

In the morning when Subedar Sher Khan opened the door of my cell at the usual time at eight he was taken aback to see me clean shaven.

"Subedar Sabeb, I've done the job myself, saving you this extra labour," I said.

"*Sala,* you're a strange man, indeed. I don't know what stuff you're made of. Now don't tell that father of yours that you have plucked your beard yourself. Otherwise that *sala* will fly at my throat. And these guards, these sons of owls-they just stood there watching the *tamasha.*"

The guard was changed. The new guard was ignorant of what had happened at night. When Major Jadun looked at my face he let out a loud laugh. "Oh, how wonderful you look like a hairless fairy. I feel like sleeping with you. O, Subedar, have his head also shaved with a machine. Make him absolutely bald. Otherwise he is going to spoil my morals.

A few minutes later the barber came and he shaved my head clean with his machine.

The barber had not finished his job when Major Jadun again appeared on the scene. "Yar, Subedar, make a Hindu sanyasi of him," he said. "Shave off his eyebrows also." The barber immediately coin plied with his orders.

Then the Major called in the men of the guard and the people from the office, to whom, to their huge amusement, he presented me as an object of fun. He laughed like mad.

"Major Saheb, it's the whirligig of time," I said. "One day it could be your turn. You must have some fear of God in your heart!"

"The real fireworks are yet to come," he said. "You must tell us who first introduced you to these two men of the Atomic Energy Commission. And when and where did you meet them first."

"Major Saheb, this is all a fabrication," I replied. "Under duress I had given about two dozen imaginary names out of whom these two unfortunate people fell in your trap. I had seen them for the first time when they were brought to me. You are wantonly trying to make a false story true. Even if you flay me alive nothing will come out of this story."

"If it comes to flaying you we shall not shirk from that. But I know you'll lay down your arms much before that stage is reached. This is a Center where even stones start speaking. And you are only an ordinary mortal."

"It's entirely upto you, Major Saheb," I said. "You can follow any course you like. But I've nothing more to tell you."

"All right, that settles it," be said with an air of finality. Then he turned to the Subedar. "Subedar Sabeb, from today increase Bhaskar's ration. Feed him one chatack powdered chillies with each principal meal. And this should continue till my next orders."

Feeding me with red chillies became a regular routine. Then started the exercise of laying me down on a slab of ice. One day I was hung up from a rope with my hands and feet firmly tied together and a live charcoal held under my hanging feet. I kept screaming with pain which only drew the Major's laughter. I was subjected to various other tortures which would boggle one's imagination. I wanted to die but I knew of no handy way of doing it.

One night I told a guard commander who ate *paans* laced with tobacco that I had a toothache and asked him to give me some tobacco. He gave me his tobacco box and told me that I could have as much of the tobacco as I wanted. I put the entire content of the box on my tongue and swallowed it down with water. My head started reeling and I kept vomitting the whole night.

The guard commander became jittery with fear and started trembling. He sent a soldier post haste to fetch the Subedar who came running on hearing what had happened. The doctor gave me some kind of mixture as an antidote which nullified the effect of the tobacco.

"I know your game!" the Subedar thundered at me. *"Sala!* you want to die with the secret locked in your heart. But don't worry. We shall give you death all right but only after extracting the secret from you."

I was hung upside down and was not taken down till my eyes became bloodshot.

I am Produced Before General Gul Hassan

It was June 19, 1970. The guard commander came into my cell and asked me to put on my clothes. In those days I used to remain naked for I had told them that I would not wear any clothes made in Pakistan. I told the guard commander that he could take me anywhere he liked in the naked state I was in. The guard commander was furious. "Don't be a fool," he cried. "I've to present you before the General Saheb. Why are you bent upon dragging me into trouble along with yourself? Just put on your clothes or I'll have to be hard on you."

I pulled out my kurta and pajama from under the folds of a blanket. They were in tatters, unfit to be worn. The guard commander reported the matter to the Subedar. He immediately sent me the uniform of Capt. Rampal who had been arrested in 1965. I was happy to wear it. They had pasted Rampal's name on his shirt collar along with his Dehra Dun Defence Academy insignia. I was handcuffed, blindfolded and marched to the Interrogation Chamber. Strangely enough, this time my heart was not pounding.

They removed my bandage and freed my hands in the presence of the General. I stood to attention and saluted the General military fashion which he acknowledged with proper decorum and asked me to take his seat in front of him.

"Well, Mister Bhaskar, perhaps you know that those who fired at one another in the war of 1965 have since gone back to their respective countries. *Insha Allah,* you may also follow them accordingly. Then tell me why have you turned your own enemy and are creating trouble for yourself and also for us? Why don't you come out with all the facts? The sooner you do it, the sooner you will be relieved of your misery. Suppose you are awarded ten years punishment out of which you spend seven years under interrogation then those seven years will not count towards your ten years imprisonment. So why don't you make the correct statement and be done with it? They will institute a case against you and award you the punishment according to the court's findings. You can go back to your country on completion of your term."

"You're right, Janab. It's now going on to be two and a quarter years since I've been undergoing this torture. I've also stayed in the Shahi Qila at Lahore. There nobody even touched me. Amrik Singh who was instrumental in getting me arrested was also there and so was my guide, Samund Singh. The authorities there recorded our statements and took action after weighing the pros and cons. Now kindly tell me, can a frail person like me dare to hide anything in the face of such persistent tortures? For more than a quarter year Major Jadun Saheb has been harping on the Atomic Energy Commission secrets, which haven't any basis in facts."

"Then why did you implicate two officers of the Atomic Energy Commission?" the General asked.

I explained the General that I had done it under compulsion. If I could get away with a lie to save myself from harassment, well, then let them have the fun. However, the fact was that I had nothing to do with these officers. But they wouldn't listen to me. They thought I was going back on what I had stated out of sympathy for those two officers. I further told the General that I used to hear their screams in my cell and if I tried to importunate with their tormentors on their behalf they would ask me why was I concerned about them? This torture had been going on for the last six months. Finally, I told the General that it was sheer stupidity to torture these two innocent persons.

At this Major Jadun glared at me as if he would gobble me up.

The General turned to Major Jadun. "Since when have you been interrogating this man?" he asked.

"Janab, for about one and a quarter years."

The General frowned. "O, *dalle ke bachche* (son of a pimp!) have a good look at this puny creature. One slap, he will go reeling and not get up for three days. And you've been working on him for over a year! And what have you got out of him. You're still at the same place where you had started from. I feel you are not intelligent enough to assume the responsibilities of our apex intelligence bureau. Hence you immediately start off for Comilla to join the Fifth East Bengal Regiment there. I'll convey my orders on the phone to the area military headquarters for your immediate transfer to Comilla. You will not be allowed to say farewell to your wife and children. The military car will straightaway take you to the airport from here." He ordered his batman to accompany the Major to the airport and to shoot him dead if he made an attempt to get down from the jeep enroute.

Still muttering, the General then turned to me. "Well, Bhaskar, we are sending you back to Lahore where you'll first have a summary court martial followed by a Field General Court martial. Now it's your luck whether you are awarded capital punishment or imprisonment for ten or twenty years. That's none of my concern."

"Very good, Janab." I was feeling exhilarated. I stood to attention and saluted him again. The guards pushed me back into my cell and locked its door.

My joy knew no bounds. I had been relieved of the torture of interrogation. Nobody would dare touch me and I would feel free even behind the bars. My prison life would be taking a new turn. It would be a comparatively comfortable jail life. No bickerings over food, no explanations called.

I must say a few words about Havaldar Abdul Rahman Khatak, who even in prison had helped me to keep up my morale. He spent most of his time in the office. When the office closed for the day and the people went away he would switch on his transistor and place it outside my cell. "Have a good time, Bhaskar!" he would say.

After I got a beating he would invariably come to console me. His love and affection were like a fountain in a desert which sprays cool, life-giving water. A good man in the real sense of the word. there was no hatred for me in his heart. I still shudder when I think of the FIC, Rawalpindi. But when I think of that angelic soul my head is bowed in gratitude.

Subedar Sher Khan

Sher Khan, a Pathan from Mianwali, blue-eyed, tall and strong and fair like an Englishman, he reminded me of Gregory Peck. In the beginning he was quite nice to me but gradually his behaviour changed towards me under the influence of Major Jadun. After my attempt at suicide he became my bitter enemy. He would have my cell opened at odd hours just to get me beaten with sticks and chains without any rhyme or reason. This would make me wild and I would abuse him filthily the moment my eyes landed on him. I knew he would not spare me in any case. I wanted to make him mad with anger so that he should kill me in a fit of passion. I did not feel happy on day that he did not beat me. I felt I had turned a masochist and he a sadist. At last he ordered his guards to keep me out of his sight whenever they saw him passing by that side.

They would lock me up in my cell but I would know from the sound of his footsteps that the Subedar was coming and I would start abusing him from inside my cell. By now he was fed up with beating me; maybe he had realised that I wanted to die at his hands and in consequence he had stopped going to his office through the *pucca* verandah. Instead he took *the kutcha* path. I often enquired from the guard commander why the Subedar had stopped visiting my cell, reminding him that I had gone without a beating for the last ten days and my bones were now itching for his kicks. "Why hasn't that son of a barber come to massage my body? Tell him that the husband of his sister is pining to meet him." The guard commander would feel incensed but according to the regulations he could not lay his hand upon me.

But when the office started he conveyed my message verbatim to the Subedar. Bursting with rage, he stormed into my cell and started kicking me right and left, making up for the omission of the last ten days my teeth shook to their roots, my lips were cut and my body was drenched in blood. Just then his batman came running to him. "Janab, your son has fallen from the roof!" he announced. The Subedar's hand remained suspended in the air. "Allah's curse on you!" he cried. "*Sala*, why do you provoke me into beating you? A mad man that you are, you are also driving me insane. I just lose my head when I see you. God has punished me for it. Look, my son has fallen from the roof!"

He ordered that I should be taken to the hospital to have my wounds dressed.

After that his attitude towards me underwent a sea change.

He would pass by me in silence. My behaviour towards him had also changed. I had stopped fulminating against him. If Major Jadun ordered him to beat me, "Yes, Janab," he would say promptly but temporise and do nothing about it.

One evening he came to me and said, "You're an educated man but why do you keep behaving like cattle? Spend your time in the worship of Allah. Remember your Bhagwan. He is merciful. Your bad days may come to an end. Don't speak about it to anybody but I'll tell you something in secret. We have not been able to extract anything from those two Atomic Energy chaps in six months. Jadun is in trouble. He doesn't know how to account for it to his seniors. In the beginning we were happy that we had caught two traitors of the country. But Major Jadun is so hasty and wilful that he does not care to listen to anyone. And so foul-mouthed that one does not want to express one's views before him. Anyway, he'll reap as he sows. Being his junior I'm not bothered. You quietly pass your days here. If you have an adequate reply to any of his questions just tell him. Otherwise just hold your peace. He is passing through a crisis and may do something desperate. He can make you the scapegoat of his own lapses."

Subedar Sher Khan went away, leaving me to my thoughts.

The same night Major Jadun came to his office at night. Through an oversight a guard had left the door of my cell open. The Major took the guard seriously to task for his lapse, cashiering him on the spot and then pushing into my cell, started beating me. Time and again he brought up the question of the Atomic Energy Commission to which I had no reply. He left me only when I fainted.

In the morning I felt as if my body was going to pieces. I narrated the incident to Subedar Sher Khan. "I had told you that his wrath was going to fall on you," he said. "But it's only a matter of days. A decision is soon to be taken about you this way or that. You must pray to your Bhagwan. He is the only one who can save you."

After that it became a regular practice with me to spend my time in meditation. Since I had taken my mind off the worries of investigation my health started improving. When I looked at my reflection in a glass of water I felt as if it was someone else's face. Its brooding sullenness had disappeared. An unknown voice kept whispering in my ear that if I was fated to breathe free air once agam these prison walls could not hold me back.

One afternoon I heared an uproar outside the jail premises. The FIC guards were trying to prevent some people from coming in, while those people were shouting at the top of their voices that the FIC had kept some of its people behind the bars and that they would not leave the place without rescuing these innocent people. Later I learnt that it was the people of the Atomic Energy Commission who had come with their own guards to rescue the two scientists. Apprehending firing on both sides Major Jadun apprised General Gul Hassan of the whole situation on the phone. At that time General Hassan was the Corps Commander of Rawalpindi and was later elevated to the position of CMC under Bhutto's regime. "They too are Pakistani," he told Major Jadun. "Let these two people go. They should only be kept under surveillance. If something incriminating is found against them we can again bring them back to the Center. I am coming over to you and shall personally examine the person who has given you the clue about these scientists."

The two persons were soon led out of their cells. Once outside the dark cells, they ran like mad as if fearing that they may again be put behind the bars. After their departure my hope of being taken out of here also revived. The new place I would be sent to would any time be better than this hell.

From Rawalpindi to Lahore

One morning the Subedar brought me a brand new green kurta and pajamas. There were also a banian and an underwear and a pair of chappals. He said, "Bhaskar, you are being taken to Lahore where they will file a case against you." At seven a station wagon arrived to take me to the Rawalpindi railway station. The guard this time belonged to the 14th Punjab Regiment now stationed at Lahore. As usual my hands were tied behind my back and a man helped me to get into the station wagon. It was a one-and-four guard, comprising of a havaldar and four guards.

Subedar Sher Khan was there to see me off. "Well, Bhaskar, Khuda Hafiz!" he said, waving me off.

At that time I never had an inkling of ironies which were in store. While leaving Rawalpindi it had never occurred to me that Providence would one day wreak vengeance from my tormentors in manners beyond fancy. Subedar Sher Khan was taken prisoner in the Bangladesh War of 1971 at Comilla Cantonment where Major Kamal Raza Judan had preceded him. This contomnent was the first to be attacked by the Mukti Bahini. Even the families of the officers were butchered. I learnt about it from the army newspaper. In those days Subedar Sher Khan was under military arrest at Meerut and he had announced on the radio about his whereabouts; "I am Subedar Sher Khan of Mianwali, Punnukhel, speaking from somewhere in India. If anyone in Pakistan hears my message he may kindly convey it to my family. I am all right here."

The Pindi Express started towards Lahore. The guard commander removed the bandage from my eyes and freed one of my hands. The guards were handsome youth and were very kind to me throughout the journey, sharing their tea and other things with me. In the compartment I was the centre of everybody's attention and in response to their enquiries it was explained that I was an army deserter being taken back to my unit. They were careful not to reveal to anybody that I was an Indian.

We reached Lahore at five in the evening. A three-tonner had come to receive us at the station from where I was driven straight to the unit's quarter guard. For the past few months I had been eating only one meal a day and fasted on Mondays and Fridays, confining myself only to a small quantity of boiled potatoes. After two months I was transferred to another quarter guard where I was kept handcuffed day and night. They had also shackled my legs with a chain.

I strongly objected to this kind of treatment because warts

had formed under my arms. I gave up eating in protest till they agreed to remove the handcuff from one of my hands. Soon after the chain was also removed from my legs. Incidentally, it was the same 13th Punjab Regiment which had run away from the battle-field. For this reason the men of this regiment had an edge against me. But since according to the regulations they could not man-handle me they just watched me in sullen silence. The parade ground was in front of the quarter guard and every morning I would watch the jawans turning out for parade.

One day the unit's Subedar, Sikander Sultan, informed me that they would soon be starting the court martial proceedings against me and that I would be chargesheeted under Section 3 of the Official Secrets Act. I waited for it each day, tense with anxiety. One night I dreamt that the jawans had driven me in a car to a deserted place surrounded by high walls. I woke up with a start, feeling greatly agitated. Would they be transferring me to the Attock Fort from where no Indian had ever come out alive? When dead they poured kerosene over his dead body and set a match to it. There was only one redeeming feature. Only persons charged under Section 32, Defence of Pakistan Rules were sent to Attock whereas I had been hauled up under Section 29 of the same Rules. But one never knew. They could change the Section anytime.

At about eleven, one day, the door of my cell was flung open. I found a havaldar and four jawans standing before me.

Was I going to appear before the court martial? But I was handcuffed and blindfolded again to be driven off in a military vehicle. Rushing along the busy roads of Lahore the vehicle abruptly came to a screeching halt. When the bandage was removed from over my eyes, I learnt to my great joy that I had been brought back to the Shahi Qila at Lahore.

My dream of those high walls had come true. I was produced before Inspector Durrani who had now been elevated to the rank of a DSP. He asked them to remove my handcuffs and offered me a chair. He was very polite to me as if he was talking with a relative on a visit.

Back to Shahi Qila

As we were talking, Raja Gul-Anar Khan came to Durrani's room. "Thank God, Bhaskar, you have saved us from ignominy," he said giving me a bear hug. "We were worrying all the time that if those Pindi people came up with something new we would find it difficult to satisfy them. But what induced you to tell them that we had not even touched your body while you were in this Qila with us? We had written to them that we had tried all possible means but had failed to get any clues from you."

I said, "Raja Saheb, one is doled out joy and sorrow as it lies in one's fate. And so I thought I had no business to tell a lie. I can never forget how kind you had been to me. You were so often in my thoughts. Why did you throw me to those wolves? You may think that they are superior to you but they are not even worthy of licking the dust off your feet. They thought of all conceivable ways of torturing me but things remained where they were. They just kept hammering at one point which absolutely made no sense. At last they thought that it was nothing but an exercise in futility and had let me alone. I don't understand why I have been brought here again."

He said, "I know they treated you shabbily and I'm really sorry for it. But we are helpless. These army blokes have the last word in everything. You'll soon know the reason why you have been brought here again. Durrani Saheb will talk to you about it. But you must be careful. Think twice before you answer his questions. Don't make any commitment which you cannot keep. Now I'll hand you over to Durrani Saheb and leave."

After he was gone Durrani Saheb turned to me. "Bhaskar, I'm sorry that you had to undergo such hardships We would be happy to release you so that you could go back to your country and work for us from there."

"Chaudhri Saheb, what's this childish talk?" I said cut to the quick. "After having tortured me for three years now you've suddenly thought of releasing me so that you can use me to serve your own ends. It's foolish of you to think in that vein. I would be a big fool to repose faith in you. And it would be equally true for you not to trust me in such matters."

He said, "Look, Bhaskar, don't wag your tongue like a fool. Here is a wonderful opportunity for you to make good in life. These Indians, as you can see, have ruined your life. Even if you are repatriated, of which I see no hope for the next fifteen years, your people will look at you with suspicious eyes. Secondly, they will consider you as dross – a worthless commodity to own at a throw-away price. The officers who have sent you here, for all I know, may even refuse to recognise you. You are living here in reasonable comfort, eating the jail food for doing nothing while back home your poor mother has to drudge for others. She has to eke out a living by cleaning others' soiled utensils. And your wife has to work in others' houses like a maid servant. And what about your son whom you haven't even seen till now? We'll give out to the world that you have escaped from jail. We will notify it in the newspapers and broadcast it over this radio. All you have to do is to write a letter home and ask your parents to come over. It could even be your wife or sister. They will stay with us as hostages. Of course, we shall treat them as our guests. After five years during which time you will no doubt be able to establish your credentials with us we shall send them back to their country."

I said, "Durrani Saheb, it sounds so alluring. But I wish it did not have the hollowness of a stage play. But who can tell whether this play will be built round the theme of escape or death. You can as well declare me, an escapee and then riddle me with a bullet. As for getting my parents or wife or sister over here to be kept as hostage, you know I can't escape the suffering or happiness which fate has decreed for me. I've already undergone great suffering. Why should I drag my people into it and wantonly punish them for no wrong done by them? No, your proposition is not acceptable to me."

Durrani was greatly peeved at my refusal. "Look, don't try to be over clever," he said. "Those of your spies who were taken prisoners in 1953 are still rotting in our jails. Your Government has not even bothered to find out what has happened to their families. Some of them are even reduced to beggary, going from door to door for a morsel of food. Have some pity on your youth and agree to what I am saying."

"Chaudhri Saheb, it seems the bright chapter of my life is over and now only darkness lies ahead of me for which I'm fully prepared. Don't be angry with me. One who is already down is free from the fear of being blotted out of existence. Your suggestion has no significance for me."

"Let's drop it at that then. You know the best. I never expected that an educated man like you could have the brain of a fool. Go back to your cell and rest."

The guard escorted me back to my room. This time I was not put in the elephant's underground cellar but in one of the rooms near the main gate where only those prisoners were kept whose interrogation had come to an end. Khoh Singh son of Faisla Singh, by a strange coincidence, was also lodged in my room. His whole body bore marks of branding. In the late hours of the night when I sat down to pray he got infuriated. "Stop this nonsense!" he cried. "The whole world is sleeping. What business have you to disturb God in his sleep. This city belongs to Allah. Your *Parmatma* cannot have his way here." He kept muttering for a long time. His main complaint was that he had been closeted with a Pandit who had first been gobbling up goats by posing as a Muslim and had then started worshipping Lord Krishna by posing as a Hindu. "What's the protector of cows doing here?" he asked me. "Go and sleep and let others also sleep."

From his demeanour and terrible voice it appeared that he had gone insane. I feared lest he should do me some physical harm and started praying wordlessly in my mind.

In the morning, when we had finished eating, he said to the sentry, "O, you specimen of the tribe of pimps, light a cigarette for me." I thought the sentry would give him a good thrashing. But nothing of the sort happened. Perhaps they were tired of beating him. He finished his cigarette in peace and then turned to me. "Brother, are you alive or dead? If you are alive why don't you talk? Why have you created this ominous atmosphere around us?"

I was eager to talk with him. "What's your real name?" I asked him by way of a start.

"*Abe O,* son of a Brahmin!" he thundered at me. "One blow of my powerful hand and your brain will spill out. My name is Khoh Singh and my father's name is Faisla Singh. How dare you question me when even these, *salas* of mine have not been able to get anything out of me? I warn you, so long you are with me, stop being personal. No more questions, you understand!"

125

I looked at him, bewildered To add to my bewilderment he gave a loud guffaw. *"Abe sale,* why are you looking so scared? Look, I won't ask you where you come from and you shouldn't ask me where I come from. Right? Remember, I'm saying this for your good. Do you know how to play *Barah Tehni* (a game akin to chess)?" When I said "Yes," he promptly broke a chip from the neck of the pitcher and draw twelve lines with it on the bare floor. The game started.

He kept taking while engaged in playing. "This game is a sister to chess," he said, "and as you must be knowing chess is a royal game, played by royalty who have nothing else to do, nor have a care in the world. They keep at it, round after round, while their servants hang around to attend to their needs. They serve them food and prepare their *hukkahs.* Our condition as you must have noticed, is very much like that of royalty. Like royalty we have nothing to do. The *khansamas* bring us our food, the water-carrier brings us water and the sentry lights cigarettes for us like a slave. Son, I doubt if you had the run of so many servants at home."

I found his observation rather amusing. It made me laugh. As the poet Ghalib has said such thoughts are good, for they divert the mind at no cost. Khoh Singh was very good at *Barah Tehni* and scored over me everytime. Much as I wished, I just couldn't beat him. Either I lost or the game ended in a draw.

Many days passed in this manner. One evening Raja Saheb told me that I would soon be presented before a magistrate to record my statement under Section 164 after which I would be sent to Kot Lakhpat Jail at Lahore.

On the morning of 27 November, 1970, 1 was handcuffed and taken in a van to the court of the first class magistrate, Sayyed Mirza Javed Dastgir. Raja Gul-Anar Khan accompanied me to the court. The statement under Section 164 was just a formality. The Raja Saheb wrote the statement according to his own fancy and asked me to sign along the dotted lines. I was taken to the Kot Lakhpat Jail at five in the evening. The Deputy Superintendent Jail, Syyed Kazini received me in the vestibule. It appeared that Raja Saheb had already told him about me. The Deputy Superintendent took me to a death cell where thirteen Indian prisoners were already lodged. Sohan Lal, who belonged to Adampur and was undergoing a term of fourteen years was the first to meet me. There were also others – Chanan Singh, Bhuller, Yunus Massih, Jacob Massih, Gulzar Singh among others. They gave me bear hugs. I looked a perfect Brahmin -shaved head, a long tuft, a turmeric mark on my forehead and a rosary round my neck. I also wore my dhoti in Pandit style. I had given up wearing a shirt although winter had set in.

I learnt from them that Amrik Singh was also lodged in a nearby cell in barrack No 12. Apart from me, he had been instrumental in getting Sohan Lal and Chanan Singh also arrested. I also learnt from them that after getting me arrested Amrik Singh had returned to Pakistan along with Shiv Kumar alias Teddy and had stayed with Major Aijaz Maqsood of the 596 FIU, Lahore. That night after receiving payment from Major Maqsood they had started gambling. Teddy lost everything, so much so that he had to part with the rings on his fingers. Then Teddy asked Amrik Singh for a loan which the latter flatly refused. Piqued, Teddy played dirty with him. He pulled out some FIU papers and hid them in an opium box which Amrik Singh had planned to smuggle out to India. Teddy informed Major Maqsood that Amrik Singh was playing a double game with Pakistan which fact could easily be established by looking into his opium box.

Amrik Singh was sleeping at that time. Major Maqsood woke him up and told him that he had come to help him across the border. Before starting, his opium box was examined and those incriminating papers were very much there. Amrik Singh was stunned. They beat him up and straightway drove him to the Shahi Qila where he was kept under interrogation for over one year.

The same night, after Amrik Singh's arrest, Major Maqsood had passed on Amrik Singh's money, which formed a substantial amount, to Shiv Kumar. By way of an additional reward he had also given Shiv Kumar one maund of opium which originally belonged to Amrik Singh. Shiv Kumar set out for the Indian border in the company of a smuggler named Mohinder Singh. They had just crossed the border when Mohinder Singh shot Shiv Kumar dead out of greed for his money and threw his body in the river.

We learnt these things from Balbir Singh who knew Shiv Kumar and Amrik Singh and was now interned in Pakistan. In this manner retribution had visited the two traitors of the country. One of them was dead and the other, Amrik Singh, was spending his days in barrack No. 12 in a most miserable condition. He was almost on the verge of mental collapse. The Indians had disowned him and the Pakistanis would have no truck with him for they too regarded him as a traitor. They said, He who cannot be true to his own country – how can he be true to us?"

Now manacled, Amrik Singh had fallen in everyone's eyes. When an easy going man has to put in hard labour it is like a veritable death to him. Such was the case with Amrilk. He would quarrel with the jail authorities complaining that he had been faithful to them and that it did not behove them to give him such a shabby deal at which he would come in for more beating.

The Indian prisoners used to have their tea together. One evening when I went to barrack No. 12 for my tea, Sohan Lal by a gesture pointed in the direction of a man who was spinning out bamboo yarn with feeble hands. "Your friend, Amrik Singh!" he whispered to me. I could not recognise him. An unkempt beard, a wrinkled face and his body which used to be so burly when I had last seen him now looked almost emaciated.

As I picked up the big pot of scalding tea to go he salaamed me. I felt like throwing the boiling tea in his face but held myself back just in time. I had no right to take the law into my own hands. I would leave it to Providence to deal with him.

His barrack was just behind our own barrack and we often heard his screams. He could not put in hard labour and therefore came in for punishment.

One day a lunatic hit him with a brick on his head but none of us took any notice of him. It appeared his sins had come to roost. He begged for death but it seemed that even death was not prepared to oblige him. It was only the first year of his imprisonment and he had a journey of years and years lying ahead of him.

Would he be able to go back to his country alive? And even if he succeeded in doing so would life be worth living? Would the Indian government spare him? Such thoughts had driven him mad. The hunter had been caught in his own net.

First Home Connection

I had come to be known as Pandit in the Kot Lakhpat Jail. The prisoners came to show me their hands and made me offerings of fruits, cigarettes and sometimes even money most of which I distributed among my fellow prisoners. These things came as a windfall to them. Among the prisoners there was a young boy of fifteen, named Liaquat, a resident of Kasur, who had been sentenced to twenty years imprisonment on charge of murder. His appeal was under consideration of the High Court. He showed me his hand. I made some calculations on the basis of numerology and told him that he would be going home within the next three months. Through his medium I sent my first letter home to which I got a reply within a week.

The letter bore the thumb impression of my son, Dhaleshwar, who was only two and a quarter years old at that time and was born four months after my arrest. I was overjoyed to get the letter particularly because it said that all was well with my people at home. I got five rupees worth of sweets through the good offices of Munsi Nazeer and distributed it among my fellow prisoners in my barrack. I also gave five rupees to that Munsi who was reluctant to take it but subsequently accepted at my insistence. We were still celebrating when news came in that Liaquat's appeal had been accepted by the High Court and he was being released. Before going he gave me a substantial quantity of sweets, besides some money, post cards and postal envelopes. This enabled me to correspond regularly with my people at home.

When Amrik Singh in barrack No. 12 learnt about my correspondence, he reported the matter to the Superintendent Jail, out of pique, maintaining that being an under-trial I was not entitled to correspond with my family. They searched me but could not find anything incriminating in my possession. I had been careful to keep such things with my Pakistani prisoner friends. The Jail Superintendent, Haji Iftkhar told me that Amrik Singh had reported against me in writing and had also sent a copy of the report to the CID. He was, therefore, helpless in the matter but was good enough to assure me that in future if there was any letter for me it would duly be passed on to me, adding that I should not make a song and dance about such letters and keep them a secret. He also cautioned me to tell my people not to allude to my letters when writing to me. "You are living in an alien country in the most trying circumstances and I can understand your plight," he said. "But when your case gets under way such restrictions upon you will be waived off."

After that I became extra cautious and did not breathe a word to any one when I got a letter. My parents' condition, as revealed by subsequent letters was none too good. But I could do nothing about it. Once out of sheer disgust I wrote to them that I would prefer not to have any letter rather than those gloomy ones describing their woes. Such letters only demoralised me instead of cheering me up when I was marking my time in the enemy's prison, anxious to know whether I would be awarded death sentence or life imprisonment. After that the tone of their letters changed.

Some inner power once impelled me to write to my mother that I hoped to come home in the course of the next four or five years. In reply my wife, Prabha, wrote to me that I should keep up my spirits. She would cheerfully wait for me till the very end of her life.

My wife's innocent face would haunt me day and night. Fate had separated us only eight months after our marriage. I would even visualise my son, whom I had never seen, standing before me and waving to me as if saying, "Papa, when will you return home?"

Now only one fear tormented me – would they pass a death sentence upon me? I would seek refuge with my God who had sustained me through an ordeal of those two and a half years in the Shahi Qila and FIC Rawalpindi. God, who had brought me out of that hell would also take me home. This faith in Him sustained me through my most trying days. The wish to be by the side of my near and dear ones also kept up my drooping spirits. Come what may I must live for them.

My Wife

A wife whom in Urdu they call the companion of one's life plays a significant role in her man's life. In the case of many great men we find the faces of their wives peeping from behind their own faces. Innumerable writers, poets, artists, scholars and leaders reached the acme of their glory only through the inspiration of their wives; if their wives were not in the background they would perhaps lose their lustre. My wife, Prabha, proved to be a great source of inspiration to me. She helped me to sustain my faith in myself.

I had first met her in Moga when I was doing my B.Ed. We married against the wishes of her parents. Her father, Shri Sat Parkash Sood, was the Chief Controller in the Railways at Dar-es-Salawn in Tanzania. Theirs was an affluent family. But I had married her and brought her home in the clothes she was standing in. I had refused to accept any dowry.

When I was imprisoned in Pakistan her parents did their best to persuade her to go away to Tanzania with them. But she strongly resisted their suggestion. So much so that she did not even go to the railway station to see them off. She said, "When my husband returns I'll gladly accompany him to Delhi to bid you good-bye at the Palam airport but till then I will not cross the threshold of our house." When I think of her I am reminded of Lakshman's wife, Urmila.

Yes, she had hopefully waited for the day of my return. Not only that. She had infused a new life in me through her inspiring letters. When her letter came I would almost cut myself off from my friends and retire into my shell. I had no time even for squabbles with the people in jail. One afternoon when I was reading my wife's letter over and over again, a fellow prisoner, Satish, would not stop pulling my leg; unwittingly he even said something nasty against me which I felt had an ominous ring. I warned him but there was no stopping him. Then I lost my patience and ran after him brandishing my kitchen knife. Although his legs were chained, he scampered off as if in a bid to save his life, shouting. "He's killing me! He's killing me!" The other prisoners came out of their barracks, out of curiosity. On such occasions the nambardars usually blew their whistles to sound the alarm but this time they only watched me in surprise for I was considered to be a sober and cool-headed person. They just stopped me in my flight and asked, "Pandi@ what's happened?" But before I could explain Satish broke down like a girl, pleading with the nambardars that they should snatch away the knife from me for his life was in danger. I could not help laughing for Satish had made quite a spectacle of himself.

When the nambardar's came to know what had transpired, they were furious. They gave Satish a few lathi blows and said, "First you create a rumpus and then whimper like a girl. *Sala!* you must be taught a lesson." They wanted to put him in the penal barrack where the prisoners are given a beating morning and evening as a matter of routine but I intervened on his behalf. This incident had one salutary effect; after this no Indian prisoner ever tried to be fresh with me.

Those Martial Law Days

I was talking of the days when Martial Law had a complete stranglehold over entire Pakistan. In every sphere the military rulers had a field day. People on the road were pulled up for trifling lapses and caned or made to pull their ears like school boys. In Lahore itself thousands of men and women were hauled up every day on the charge of riding two to a bike and ordered to tweak each other's ears or do a hundred sit-ups each before the public gaze. In order to perpetuate his military rule Yahya Khan was brazenly postponing general elections from time to time. In consequence, public demonstrations and strikes by the disgruntled people had become the order of the day. To counter such moves the government had established mobile military courts which sentenced the offenders on the spot. By way of punishment the culprits were publicly whipped or had to pay heavy fines.

In those days Cheema was the Martial Law Administrator. His forefathers, he claimed, were Sikhs. He used to tell each undertrial as he was produced in his court, "You must know this is the court of Ranjit Singh. I'll blow you to pieces!"

Once when the court was about to rise for the day a case of a village feud over a *peepul* tree was brought before the court. The police inspector rushed in just in time "Janab, there's a *peepul* tree……" he said panting for breath.

Without hearing him further Cheema Saheb pronounced, "It's all right. Bring the *peepul* in the court tomorrow morning." And he walked out of the court room. The police inspector was at his wit's end. He did not know how to get over this quandary. He went to the village at night, had the tree cut down into pieces and brought it to the court compound early in the morning in truck.

When the police inspector appeared in Cheema's court the exalted personage asked him, "Have you brought the *peepul?*"

"Yes, hazoor," the inspector replied.

"Then why don't you produce it in the court?"

"Janab, it's lying cut in the court compound."

Cheema Saheb was annoyed. "You are a good-for-nothing police inspector!" he exclaimed. "Why did you allow it to be cut down? Couldn't you protect it even for one night? Now you have come to me with its corpse."

"Janab, it's not a man, it's a tree to which two contending parties have staked their claims. According to the Janab's orders I've brought the tree in a truck."

"You foolish man, why didn't you tell me before? You're

responsible for wasting the court's precious time. Yahya Saheb is right when he says that you civilians are unfit to run the government. Go out and line up the disputing parties. How many are they?"

"Therty-two people, Janab. Fifteen on one side and seventeen on the other."

"All right, do as I tell you. I'll be there presently." When Cheema Saheb came out of the court, the two parties lined up on both sides of the truck, were ready for his inspection.

Cheema Saheb sent for eight men of the guard and asked them to take charge of the contending parties.

"Well, jawans, four of you go with one party and four with the other," he ordered. "These parties will carry half the tree each on their heads and march to their village. If anyone of them stops on the way for a breather give him ten kicks on the spot. And Police Inspector Saheb, you will follow them on a bicycle. If any of these jawans fail to carry out my instructions remove his belt there and then. I'll myself deal with the fellow. Now, one, two, three, quick march! This is my way of dispensing justice."

The feuding villagers were in real trouble. They had to march kilometres to reach their village, carrying heavy loads on their heads.

Such whimsicalities were a common occurrence in Cheema Saheb's court. A sweetmeat seller was challaned for mixing water in his milk. Cheema Saheb ordered that his nose should be held under water every alternate minute and this process should continue till the rising of the court. After that he should go to his shop rubbing his nose on the road.

Such grotesque punishments had a salutary effect on the public and brought down the crime rate. But on the other hand, the army people, intoxicated with power misused their authority and resorted to mean practices. Particularly those who held high ranks in the army used their positions to settle old scores with their enemies. There was no one to question their autocratic ways.

However, there was no denying the fact that the nation could not be brought on the path of rectitude without the promulgation of Martial Law in view of the fact that a large part of the population was living on crime or on the earnings of its women. The crass misuse of the institution of four marriages was nowhere more apparent than in Pakistan; not in any other Islamic country, much less in India which too had a large Muslim population. In Pakistan many had demeaned themselves by lowering this institution to the level of a regular profession. Of the four wives, the husband kept one in Lahore, the second in Multan, the third in Lyallput and the fourth in Sialkot. Then posing as a traveling salesman, the husband would go from one wife, to another, grabbing up their nightly earnings. If any one of them refused, pat came the divorce. It was very easy to seek divorce.

In the name of *mehar* to seal the marriage, the bride was

entitled to eleven or fifty one rupees from her husband. In rich families the *mehar* even went as high as a lakh of rupees. But it was the girls of the poor families who became the target for exploitation. Their husbands went out hunting for customers for their wives and lived on their incomes.

Crime is rampant in Pakistan and manifests itself in many ususual forms. There are charlatans who pose as *pirs* and are surrounded by devotees. People come to them to have their currency notes duplicated. The 'Dabba' *pir* has made a great Dame for himself in this line. The day he was arrested his 'exploits' became the front page news of all the newspapers.

These *pirs* are quite a spectacle to watch. They fill their *chelums* with *charas* (hemp) and abuse the people while taking long pulls at their *chelums*. They even make a show of attacking them with their long tongs. The filthier their abuses and the more they put their devotees on the run, the more 'heavenly', that is nearer to God, they are considered to be.

Kasur's Karamat Ali Shah who was known as 'Nara Pir' had won great renown. He had tied a pajama string to a peg in the wall of his room. There was a stream of women waiting outside to make obeisance to him. He would call them in one by one and if he took a fancy to a beautiful woman he would ask her to unknot the pajama string. If the innocent woman, not knowing what the man's game was, proceeded to untie the string of her *salwar* he would beam and at once go for her. But if she objected he would glare at her and denounce her for having a dirty mind. He would say that all be had asked her was to untie the knot of the pajama string hanging from the peg which symbolised the knot in her future fate. He would become so angry that the woman would start trembling in fear and as per hints thrown by the *pir* she would promise to bring a hen and a big pot of *zarda* the following Thursday to atone for her sin. Soon his 'doings' were unmasked and he came in for a big thrashing at the hands of the people. His face was blackened and he was taken round the city on a donkey. After that he was never seen in Kasur.

In Pakistan people keep arms illegally and that is one of the reasons why there is so much crime in that country. Beyond Peshawar there is a place called Landi Kotal where one can see foreign pistols lying piled up in heaps and on open sale. Most of the weapons one sees with the people in Punjab are bought from that place and a substantial part of these weapons is smuggled out to India. A pen-like pistol, holding one bullet sells at a hundred rupees a piece. Every house in Lahore boasts of possessing an unlicenced arm. Even three military regimes have not succeeded in stamping out this bane. It is evident that if people can have easy access to such lethal weapons they wil' not hesitate to go on the rampage on tie slightest pretext. There is lot of arm-twisting going on every where. People loot shops in broad daylight while the police looks the other way. The police is in the pay of the goondas.

The Pakistani Muslims are great religious fanatics. In this

regard the Indian Muslims are only their pale shadows. In our country, the Muslim hand goes up more in wielding a weapon that in saying a prayer. But in Pakistan the Muslims are extremely regular in saying their namaz. The offices close every Friday so that the people can congregate to hear the religious sermon. The month of Ramzan is something unique in as much as all the hotels and restaurants remain closed in daytime. To eschew fasting or abetting in its observance is considered to be a crime and those guilty of such lapses are subjected to whipping. In the evening people visit one another, carrying oranges and salt for the purpose of breaking the fast. Fasting which is considered to be a very pious act starts and ends to the sound of a siren which, as it happens in wartime, goes off punctually every morning and evening throughout the month of Ramzan. When the Eid moon is sighted, joy is expressed with the boom of guns. The Shahi Masjid of Lahore is famous for the celebration of Eid.

I don't deny that they have religious factions in Pakistan. Clashes between shias and Sunnis during Muharram are not uncommon. Sometimes things get out of control and the army has to be called in. The Muharram is seen at its best in Multan where the Shias form themselves into caravans and march wearing the dress of mourning and shouting 'Ya Hasan, Ya Hussain' to the beating of breasts. Many wear chains stuck with knives and scourge themselves with these chains, shouting 'Ya Ali!' and drawing blood which flows down from their breasts in rills. The roads from which the procession passes are covered with blood.

The Sunnis however, look askance at these practices of the Shias, maintaining that Hasan and Hussain, the grandsons of the Prophet attained martyrdom in the name of Islam and to mourn for them in this manner amounts to tarnishing their fair names. Hence they express their disapproval by throwing stones at the processions which leads to clashes, marked by free use of knives, lathis and even guns on both sides. It is a hey-day for the goondas. In the prevailing confusion they freely indulge in arson and looting.

The condition of the Mirzai Musalmans is worse than that of the Shias. Both the Shias and the Sunnis hold them in contempt. The Prophet of the Mirzai Musalmans hailed from Qadian in the Indian territory of Punjab where he had established his own heaven and hell'. His followers are known as 'Mirzais'. In 1968 a *jehad* was launched against the as and the Jamait-e-Islam, Pakistan, forced the government to proclaim that no Mirzai would be given a government job, nor would be be entitled to excercise his franchise. If a was found dining with a Muslim at the same table the latter would get up from the table without eating and force the Mirzai to sit at a separate table.

Still worse is the plight of the Deendar Muslims who constitute the sweeper and the water-carrier classes. In the first place they suffer from an actue inferiority complex and their children are forced to follow their traditional vocation. In the second place they are denied the facilities which are generally available to their counterparts in India. They dare not sit along with the upper class Muslims. The live by manual labour, skinning dead animals and trading in bones. It is rare for a Deendar Muslim to attain some high position. The bulk of them spend their lives grovelling before the upper class sheikhs.

The Syyed Musalmans who claim to be the descendants of the Holy Prophet's family exploit their position most shamelessly. They are said to have the inherent right to claim by force girls of the other castes though no one outside their caste dares look at their girls. A Syyed may be an inveterate profligate or a bad character yet he is held in esteem. They make talismans and receive votive offerings. If someone utters even a word against a Syyed he is supposed to atone for it in accordance with a prescribed procedure. It is considered a sin not to carry out a Syyed's behest. Even murders are committed at their instance and houses raged to the ground. In spite of such sacrileges to raise a voice against a Syyed amounts to a revolt against the Holy Prophet himself which would cast a Muslim into hell after death. Even if a Muslim's existence on earth is no better than a perpetual hell he can't even contemplate such a harrowing eventuality. The Syyeds take full advantage of these gullible people. Creating before them the illusion of an imaginary Heaven they loot these illiterate people with both hands, making their lives worse than hell.

In the Midst of Death Cells

There are thirty-two death cells in the Kot Lakhpat Jail of which the three at one end were occupied by Indian prisoners. Three to five condemned prisoners each were consigned to the remaining cells. Every day a prisoner found his way to the gallows and a new prisoner came to take his place. Instead of decreasing, their number kept on going up. Most of them were prisoners whose appeals had been turned down by the High Court or the Supreme Court, or in some cases their mercy petition was under consideration of the President who as statistics showed turned down more than 80% of such petitions. To everybody's surprise even though in the jaws of death these doomed prisoners laughed hilariously. They sang and shouted 'Ya Ali!' to maintain the illusion of their manliness till death claimed them.

I saw very few prisoners wailing or shedding tears before mounting the gallows. Only those who claimed to be innocent and complained of miscarriage of justice wept and there were others who shed tears for their young wives. On some days six prisoners were executed together at a time. A condemned prisoner was notified a day in advance when his relatives were allowed to meet him for the last time. The gallows were enclosed by a high wall on all sides and the prisoner awaiting his final call was kept in cell No. 32 which was nearest to the gallows. If there were more than one prisoner they were kept in the adjoining cells which were vacated by the other prisoners for this specific purpose. Some prisoners would lose their balance of mind and start raving. But their number was very small.

One day six prisoners, named, Saida, Anwar, Battu, Sarwar and two more, all hailing from Hanjarwal, a village in Lahore district who had been condemned to death were brought to the jail under police escort.

Saida had great enmity against his cousin, an uncle's son. There had been a family feud between them, leading to considerable bloodshed. One day Saida went to his cousin's house along with his two brothers' two sons and a nephew. They surrounded his cousin's house from all sides and set it ablaze after pouring kerosene over it. Anyone who tried to escape was shot dead. His cousin's nephew's wife was carrying. She was Saida's sister's daughter. She fell at Saida's feet and begged him to spare her, for she was closely related to him. But the stone-hearted Saida refused to relent. "He said, The child in your womb is our potential enemy. I'm not prepared to take any risk." Saida caught her by her arms while Anwar held her by her legs and threw her into the raging fire. In this manner they did eleven persons to death.

Two children, aged five and seven, who had hid themselves in a big jar meant for storing wheat were discovered at the time of clearing the rubble. They were lying in a swoon in the jar due to the effect of the acrid smoke. Subsequently, they were produced as eye witnesses to this carnage. Saida and his companions were charged with the murder of eleven people which also included the unborn child in its mother's womb who never saw the light of day.

Saida and his accomplices were sentenced to death and were locked up in our barrack to await their ends. Of these, Sarwar, a youth of twenty-two was the handsomest of all. In fact I have never seen such a handsome youth in my life. Even on the day of death one did not see a sign of grief on his face. On the fateful morning they were bathed and led to the gallows at four where they were all lined up and hanged three at a time. Sitting in our cells we kept hearing their cries of 'Ya Ali!' till the noose tightened round their necks and their voices were stilled for ever. Outside the jail their wives and children had kept wailing the whole night. The next day the prisoners' dead bodies were handed over to their relatives.

Another notorious criminal who was hanged while I was in jail was name Mohammed Sadiq alias 'Zachchi Ghut'. He had been sentenced to death on the charge of lifting small children. This crime has now been wiped out from Pakistan because of

151

the exemplary punishments meted out to the culprits, the punishment under Section 264-A ranging from 14 years to death sentence. This fellow Mohammed Sadiq used to visit fairs, wearing a police inspector's uniform. He would pick up the children who had strayed from their parents, giving them the assurance that they would be restored to their parents. In this manner he had lifted 250 children whom he had sold off to beggars and the more handsome ones among them to the Pathans across the frontier. The beggars would maim or blind these children and put them to begging. To arouse the sympathy of the people these beggars would go to the extent of hideously disfiguring the faces of these small children. Most of the children were kept in underground cellars and were not taken out of their hiding till they had grown out of recognition. They were then taught pick-pocketing. In this manner these kids became entirely dependent on these criminals and kept filling their pockets.

In Lahore beggars have their own 'beats' or areas which are auctioned off by goonda sardars. As already said, the more beautiful of these children were sold to the Pathans who on growing up served as their 'boys' to satisfy their carnal passions. To keep a 'boy' is considered to be a matter of great prestige among the Pathans. A Pathan who does not have a 'boy' goes down in the esteem of others.

Mohammed Sadiq who had aroused the suspicion of a CID man was caught red-handed at a fair while decoying a child.

The CID man shadowed him to his house where twenty more children were discovered underground. Sadiq was awarded capital punishment and wept like a coward when being led to the gallows, asking for mercy in vain. If only such drastic punishment could be meted out to child-lifters in India it would go a long way in stamping out this diabolical crime.

Achcha Pahalwan

Mohammed Ashraf alias 'Achcha Pahalwan', the director of the famous Pakistani film, Mangli, was undergoing a twenty years, imprisonment in the Kot Lakhpat Jail. He had been hauled up for homicide. His brother Mohammed Akmal alias 'Akka Pahalwan', who was also in the same jail had been awarded capital punishment. Achcha Pahalwan was very kindly disposed towards the Indian prisoners; he was particularly kind to me. When he saw me going about bare-foot in winter he arranged to buy a pair of shoes for me from the market. He was a saintly man. His brother had been in jail only for a few days when the orders for his execution came. Achcha Pahalwan came running to me.

"Panditji," he importunated with me, "please pray to your Bhagwan that my brother may be saved from death. I've full faith in you."

"Achcha Pahalwan, of what use can I be to you when I'm myself bound hand and foot?" I replied.

He read me a couplet to the effect that faith could even

change one's fate. It could even break iron chains from one's feet.

"I'm fully convinced that you have faith in God," he added. "That's why I've come to you."

I said, "Achcha Pahalwan, take me to your brother. I would like to have a look at him."

Achcha Pahalwan immediately called the chief warden, Rafiq Shah, who opened my cell and personally conducted me to Akmal.

Mohammed Akmal had almost lost his balance of mind.

"Come, Panditji," he welcomed me. "Nobody can hang me. If it comes to that, I'll break the iron grill! and run away to your country with you."

"Akmal Pahalwan, may I look at your palm for a minute?"

I noticed that his life-line had broken at the age of forty and then rejoined.

"Achcha Pahalwan, life and death are in God's hands," I said. "But as I can see from his hand this man will live up to the age of eighty. God can perform miracles. I think his life will be saved."

"Panditji, you know he is scheduled to be hanged at four in the morning. Even his appeal for mercy has been turned down by the President. The dice is heavily loaded against him. But I've faith in you."

We were still talking when Achcha Pahalwan's favourite sister,

Nurjahan, the Queen of Music and one of the greatest personalities of the Pakistani film world arrived along with her sixth husband, Mohammed Yusuf.

She said "Bhaijan, I just dropped in to tell you that I'm flying to Islamabad to meet President Yahya Khan. I'm going there specifically to seek his pardon for Bhaijan Akka Pahalwan. I can assure you, come what may, I'll save him from the gallows."

Nurjahan, the heart-throb of millions, left without a further word, her sixth husband, Yusuf Khan, a handsome youth in tow. It was rumoured that he had married her just to build his career in the film world and to inherit her immense wealth.

Nurjahan was fifty but looked thirty. She had recently returned from England after having overhauled her body through plastic surgery. Looking at her, even angels would have fallen for her. When I learnt that she was making a trip to Islamabad in order to meet Yahya Khan I was convinced that she would not fail in her mission. I had heard a lot about Yayha Khan's romantic nature. He was fond of wine and women. How he kow-towed to the Pakistan's notorious prostitute General Aklim Akhtar Rani, almost rubbing his nose at her threshold was known to all. I will say something about it in a subsequent chapter.

A man like him would have gone all out to please a person like Nurjahan whose body seemed to be cast in a divine mould. To obtain a pardon for somebody from a man like Yahya Khan was the easiest of jobs for her.

I said to Achcha Pahalwan, "Ashraf Bhai, the divine miracle I was alluding to has already happened. Rest assured, before the clock strikes one your brother's death sentence would have been commuted."

As I have written before Achcha Pahalwan had a soft comer in his heart for the poor prisoners and especially for the Indian prisoners. He would take pains to probe their minds and satisfy their needs as best as he could. If he came across a prisoner shivering with cold he would immediately offer him his shawl without considering its cost. Every prisoner was fond of him. His brother Akmal was, however, just his opposite; cantankerous and a man of questionable morals. But being Achcha Pahalwan's brother everybody wished well for him and wanted him to be saved from the gallows.

That day we were locked up at six in our cells and a special guard was posted outside Akka Pahalwan's cell. He was to be hanged at four the following morning. My sleep had deserted me and I was sitting near railing, waiting for someone to tell me that Akka Pahalwan had been granted the President's pardon. At twelve the prison doctor came and conducted Akka Pahalwan's routine medical examination. And then came the Maulvi of the jail to give the condemned prisoner his last sermon.

The clock stuck the hour of one. Just then I saw the

nambardar Nazir running towards my cell. "Panditji," he cried, "Achcha Pahalwan has sent sweets for you. Akka Pahalwan's death sentence has been commuted."

I was overjoyed at the news. Though one another's worst enemies we were still tied by the bond of humanity. In that jail we were neither Hindus nor Muslims. We were only hapless humans caught in the coils of our own actions.

Pir Sadaq Shah and Mullah Muzaffar

Within the four-walls of the jail there are some personalities who despite being the denizens of the jail have no respect for the jail Regulations. They can't withstand oppression of others. Mullah Muzaffar and Pir Sadaq Shah were such birds, who were very thick with each other and even the jail staff was afraid of them. Both of them had about 100 cronies each dancing to their tunes, always ready to do and die for them.

The jail people had started putting the Indian prisoners to hard labour far beyond their physical capacity. Since they fell short of the required quota they come in for a beating every day. Only three days had passed when Mullah Muzaffar came to know about the highhanded manner in which we were being treated. Brandishing his knife and hurling abuses at the jail staff he barged into our barrack, at which the jail staff scampered off. One of the jail staff blew his whistle which was a cue for the alarm bell to be sounded. When Sadaq Shah learnt what was going on in the jail he also appeared on the scene. He promptly climbed up the jail roof along with his cronies and soon the jail started resounding with the cries of 'Ya Ali!'

The Deputy Superintendent who had rushed out with his guard was dumb-founded at this turn of events. "What are you people doing in this barrack?" he demanded of Mullah Muzaffar.

"I won't stand these foreign prisoners being treated in this ghastly manner," he replied. "Why do you make them work beyond their capacity? You must have some fear of God in your hearts. And tell me, why do you beat them every day? You are doing it for the past three days."

"Who told you that?"

"Why ask me? Better ask your Chief Warden who filches money from the rich Pakistani prisoners. In addition to their own work, these Indian prisoners have also to do the work of these Pakistani prisoners."

The Chief Warden's face turned pale. But Chaudhri Aqueel, the Deputy Superintendent who had got the hang of the whole thing tried to save the situation. He asked Mullah Muzaffar and Sadaq Shah to go back to their barracks and assured them that such a thing would not happen again.

After things had quietened down the Chief Warden came to the Indian prisoners.

"You are all a bloody rotten lot!" he said. "Shirkers and do-nothings! You have nothing to do but wander all over the place. Let me see how you do it now. You filch cigarettes from one and tea from the other. I've never come in your way. But not any more. I'll work you to death."

He went away, instructing the nambardar to keep us locked in our cells and to see to it that we did not hob-nob with any outsider.

It was the daily practice with some of our Indian prisoners to visit Mullah Muzaffar and Sadaq Shah in their barrack and partake of *bhang* with them over gossip sessions. That day when the Indian prisoners did not turn up till ten, Mullah Muzaffat went out to enquire. When the nambardar refused to unlock the door of the Indians' barrack, the Mullah slapped the nambardar, sent his cap flying and snatched away the key from him. "*Sala*, if you breathe a word of it to the Chief Warden I'll poke this knife into your guts!" he threatened the nambardar.

While the nambardar watched in stunned silence, Mullah marched off with four Indian prisoners.

After some time when the Chief Warden came on his daily round and took a tally of the prisoners he found four of them missing. He came down heavily on the nambardar. Scared out of his skin, the nambardar told him the whole story.

In the evening when the defaulting prisoners returned, the Chief Warden, who was quitely waiting for them with half a dozen nambardars, threw the prisoners on the ground and gave them a good shoe beating. Then he sent for the jail barber to have their heads shaved. He also announced that he would make these fellows work on the grindstone to grind corn.

Meanwhile, Mullah Muzaffar got wind of the whole thing and he promptly appeared on the scene. At the sight of him the nambardars ran away, leaving the Chief to deal with the situation. He could do nothing but glare at Mullah.

"There is a limit to everything," Mullah thundered at the Chief Warden. "You shouldn't behave so shamelessly. Only yesterday I made you grovel before me and not a day has passed when you are again at your old game. What good does it do you to harass these poor people? Do you think I'm not a Pakistani? Am I not a Muslim? Don't I love my country? But there is some such thing as humanity too. These people are already being punished for their crime. Why add to their suffering? They will go away with the notion that the Muslim officers are a degraded lot. I know the Indian prisoners who come to me are on fatigue duty. It is only after they have swept and washed the floor of my barrack that I allow them to sit with me. If I give them something to eat why does it give you tummy ache? Get yourself transferred to some other jail or change your behaviour. if you don't, I'll set one of my roughs upon you who will beat you out of shape and you will forget that you were a somebody here."

The Chief Warden listened to him like a lamb. Nothing untoward happened for a month. Then one bight we came to know that Mullah Muzaffar was being transferred to some other jail. He was unexpectedly called in the vestibule and entrusted to the guards who took him away from the jail.

Now only Sadaq Shah and Aliyas were left behind who missed no opportunity of harassing the jail staff. One evening they refused to be shut up in their cells and ran towards the vestibule firing pistol shots in the air. The guards fired in return. That made them retreat back to their cells.

But the guards did not forgive them. Still firing, they entered Sadaq Shah's barrack. Sadaq Shah and his companions, numbering five, three of whom were in one cell and the other two in the adjoining cell, kept firing from within their cells. As a last resort the guards had to punch holes in the roof and fire upon them from above. Aliyas was the first to be killed. Sadaq Shah took shelter under his dead body and watched his other companions being ticked off one by one. Thinking that all of them had been killed, the guards descended into the cell along with their *darogha*. They were dragging out the dead bodies of the victims when Sadaq stood up suddenly and raised his arms in surrender. The Chief Warden wanted to kill him but the Superintendent did not agree.

Sadaq Shah was still an under-trial. He had a running feud with the smuggler Anwar Jhedu who had stabbed Sadaq's brother Nukra to death in the Borstal Jail at Lahore. He was now an under-trial and his case was going on in a court at Lahore.

One day Sadaq was returning from the court when some members of Jhedu's party waylaid him a few yards from the jail gate and dragged him out of the taxi. The guards who were in the taxi with Sadaq ran away in panic, leaving their guns behind. Sadaq whose legs were chained was severely handicapped and could not make a bid for escape. He was thrown to the ground and sprayed with a sten gun.

When the Indian prisoners got the news of his death their chapatis fell from their hands. They remained in mourning for a number of days. Their protectors were gone. One of them was dead. But the other must still be roaring like a lion in some otherjail as a saviour of the oppressed and the helpless.

Prof. Shahzad Jalandhari

That day I saw Sohan Lal talking with an educated Muslim prisoner. When the man was gone I asked Sohan Lal who he was. Sohan Lal got into a long harangue: "In every big city of Pakistan one would come across women in large numbers on the roads, at bus stands, in brothels and in private houses who are out to sell their bodies. Despite such easy accessibility to women, of all the countries of Asia, homosexuality is most prevalent in Pakistan. The practice of keeping 'gigolos' or 'boys' first started in the land of the Pathans and gradually spread to Sind, Baluchistan, Punjab and all over Pakistan. Seventy per cent of the men of the army are prey to it. Among the Pathans, one who does not have a 'boy' loses in prestige. Every rich Khan keeps his 'boy' lavishly decked out and embellished like girls – long curly hair, a black streak of *kajal* across his eyes. So much so; that even murders would take place on account of 'boys'. A Khan may leave his wife alone, but he would never keep his 'boy' out of sight. Even while saying his namaz he would make him sit at some distance from him. He is always assailed by the fear lest some one may elope with his 'boy' Because of this dirty habit twenty-five per cent of the people suffer from venereal diseases, so it is said."

As I learnt, this Prof. Shahzad Jalandhari of Lahore was one such romantic soul. He had taken fancy to a young son of a Colonel. One day he saw the boy coming out of the school and he lost his heart to him. He patted his check, said some nice words to him, asked him his address and gave him his own. Then he took the boy to a restaurant and entertained him lavishly. Children are hungry for affection and this innocent child could not see the devil that was peeping out of the man's heart. They started meeting every day. All the time the Professor was thinking of how to have his way with the boy.

One day the boy left home in the morning and did not return till ten at night. The Colonel's jeep raced through all the roads in search of the boy. At last he managed to get the Professor's address from a friend of his son. When the Colonel reached the Professor's house he found both the Professor and his son missing. They returned at one o'clock in a three-wheeler after a late night movie. The Colonel's batman who had stayed behind to keep watch over the house asked the boy to accompany him home but the boy refused, saying that he would come in the morning. The Colonel, terribly annoyed, rushed back in his jeep. The Professor said, "Your boy is very fond of me. I take great interest in his studies and therefore, sometimes he sleeps in my house."

The Colonel did not want to create a scene at that time and quietly took his son home. He gave him a few slaps and the boy spilled the beans. The boy told his father that the Professor had habituated him to some kind of pills and when he started dozing he did things with him. The Colonel drove straight to the police station with his son and filed an FIR against the Professor under Section 368-A of the Pakistan Criminal Code which related to the abduction of minors and under this section one can even get capital punishment.

Before the night was over the Professor was brought to the police station in handcuffs and after being given a good beating was put in the lock-up. Before leaving, the Colonel asked the Officer-in-charge of the police station to keep playing on the young man's body as on a drum.

In those days Professor Shahzad's maternal uncle, a Major in the army, was the Martial Law Administrator of Lahore. The next morning he crashed into the police station and finding the shape his nephew was in he took the police officer severely to task. He said it was for the court to deal with his nephew's case. Who was be to take the law into his own hands? "Touch him and see what happens!" he said. "I'll get you relieved from your job on the spot."

The Police Officer took the Professor out of the lock-up, got hot water for his bath, offered him a chair and sent for a nice breakfast for him. The Major was mollified. He shook hands with the Police Officer before departing and asked him to take special care of his nephew.

Fifteen minutes after the Major's departure the telephone bell rang. The man at the other end asked how Shahzad was fairing.

"He's fine, Janab," the Police Officer replied. "He's sitting in a chair in front of me and smoking. Would you like to talk to him?"

To his surprise, the Police Officer heard a shower of abuses coming from the other end. "You son of an owl, how dare you defy my orders? Last night I had told you to flay him and here you are blithely offering him a chair to make himself comfortable. I'm directly coming to the police station to give you a bit of my mind."

A few minutes later the Colonel arrived and saw Shahzad hanging upside down. "But you told me something different," he said

"Janab, I thought it was his uncle's phone. He is the Martial Law Administrator of Lahore. I've kept him hanging all night. If you allow me I'll take him down now."

"No, let him keep on hanging for sometime more," the Colonel said "I'll phone you back."

The Colonel was gone only fifteen minutes when the phone rang again. "How is Shahzad faring?" the man at the other end asked.

The Police Officer replied with aplomb, "Janab, he is still hanging upside down. And I've assigned two men to give him a good licking. May I give you the phone so that you can regale yourself with his musical voice?"

The voice at the other end thundered at the Police Officer, "You son of a swine, I'll have your police station set aflame. Didn't I tell you to be nice to him? I'm coming over right now to knock some sense into your stupid brain."

The Police Officer sat looking into vacancy utterly bewildered, holding his head between his hands. Then he said to Shahzad, "Look, Shahzad Saheb, my job is in your hands. Please save me. Tell your uncle that I've been very nice to you. Here, have a cigarette and make yourself comfortable in the chair"

When the Major arrived he was pleased to see his nephew sitting in the chair. "What rot were you talking on the phone?" he asked the Police Officer,

"Janab, may the liar's mouth be stuffed with dust. Hazoor, you can verify for yourself. I thought it was that son of an owl, the Colonel on the phone. I had to say something different just to save my skin."

Satisfied, the Major shook hands with the Police Officer and went away.

Without losing any time the Police Officer deputed two constables to take Shahzad to the District Court and firmly told them not to bring the fellow back to the police station under any circumstances. He advised them to get a judicial remand for him, if the circumstances so warranted and send him to jail. He was a pain his neck and was the last person he ever desired to see. The Colonel would insist on his being hung up while the Major would ask him to be freed.

"If the fellow is coming back tell me in advance on the phone and I'll immediately proceed on leave," the Police Officer instructed the constables.

A case was started against Shahzad. The boy's statement left no scope for ambiguity. The only redeeming feature was that on account of his uncle, Shahzad was saved from the gallows and was awarded fourteen years' rigorous imprisonment.

The Hapless Bengali: Aqueel Rahman

This unfortunate Indian had come to Pakistan on a passport valid for only six months. But as luck would have it he could never go back. He took a job in a goldsmith's shop at Lahore. Ebony black, a hideous face and an outlandish body – there was nothing about him that was not repellant and yet the goldsmith's wife, Anima Begum had fallen in love with him. They would send the goldsmith away from the shop on one pretext or other and then have a gay time in his absence. The goldsmith had become a thorn in their eyes and left to themselves they would have done away with him.

One night when the goldsmith was sleep. Anima tightly held his hands and Aqeed Rahman slit his belly. When his body turned cold Anima raised an alarm that some dacoits had murdered her husband and cleaned up the safe of all the valuables and jewellery. The investigating Inspector had a brainwave and he included the Bengali in his investigation. Four powerful blows and the timid fellow came out with the facts.

Amina Begum went one better than him. She lured the Inspector into sleeping with her and thus steered clear of all charges. On the other hand the Bengali was dragged deeper into the mire and charged with the murder of the goldsmith.

Amina met the Bengali in the lock-up and casting her feminine spell on him tutored him into making the statement that she was in no way involved in her husband's murder. In return she promised to meet all his legal expenses and assured him that she would get him scot free. That was the time when Mujib's star was in the ascendancy in Bangladesh and the Pakistanis considered all Bengalis serpents in their sleeves. The case came up before a Martial Law Court. Amina Begum did her best to have Aqueel Rahman acquitted. But as facts came to light later it was a highly tangled skein.

In fact Amina did not love Aqueel but another youth of her lane. But that handsome youth lacked the guts to do away with her husband and Amina cunningly enticed Aqueel into murdering her husband. When he was sentenced to death Ameena often came to meet him in jail. Her paramour who passed for her brother also accompanied her on these visits. Amina was extremely beautiful and when she visited the jail the prisoners, specially those under death sentence, would keep gaping at her extraordinary beauty and wonder what made her fall for this baboon. It was the paradox of the beauty and the beast.

"Aqueel, how did you manage to seduce her?" they would

ask the Bengali.

Aqueel would reply with passion. "My good friends, her husband lacked the manhood to satisfy the raging fire in her. When she saw my hefty body she knew at once that that was the answer to her lust and she fell for me. She would keep hovering round me while I was working in the shop; she would give me a sly wink or playfully pinch my arm. The matters reached a stage when I just couldn't resist her. One day when her husband was not in the shop she came in and asked me where he was. I pointed towards the inner room. As soon as she entered the inner room I followed her in and grabbing her by her arm flattened her on the ground. I had her for an hour and a half. Oh, what a heavenly time we had. From that time she became my bond slave. I don't mind mounting the gallows now. She gave me a jolly good time. Don't you see how beautiful she is? Beautiful like a fairy!"

But the poor fellow did not know how he had been duped. One evening I had just returned from the court where I had gone in connection with the hearing of my case when the Bengali beckoned me. His cell was on the way to my cell. "Pandit, I want to leave these two hundred rupees on trust with you," he said. "I'm going to be hanged tonight. But I've still hope. If my life is saved I'll take back the money from you or you can spend it in the manner you like."

I took the money from him. But later on it occurred to me that I had not done the right thing by accepting it. Maybe he would think I wanted him to die so that I could keep his money. I could not put the thought out of my mind the whole night. And then another miracle happened.

At midnight a message came from the jail office. That his execution had been stayed for a few days. Aqueel was an Indian citizen and he could not be executed without prior information to the Indian Ambassador. And then we learnt that the hangman had suddenly taken ill and the execution had to be shifted to some other date.

The following day Amina Begum came to meet him in jail and told him that she wanted to go and meet President Yahya Khan to plead for mercy on his behalf. The only snag was that she did not have money for the journey. I returned Aqueel his two hundred rupees. The other prisoners also contributed according to their means. In this manner Aqueel was able to collect about fifteen hundred rupees. Amina Begum took the money and went away with her so-called brother.

She had told Aqueel that she would be making an air dash to Islamabad and let him know by a telegram the result of her meeting with the President. But four days passed and there was no letter from her, much less a telegram. On the fifth day the jail authorities received the final orders for Aqueel's execution and he was to be hanged that night. Aqueel kept rising on his heels to watch out for Anima's arrival. But I felt that Amina had once again diddled Aqueel and told him so. The other prisoners were also inclined to agree with me. But Aqueel was still hopeful. "No, no, Pandit, she can't betray me like this," he asserted.

Incidentally, just then a brother of one Mohammed Sadaq who had been condemned to death came to meet him in jail. He was requested to go post haste to Amina's house and find out how the matter stood. The news that Sadaq's brother brought was most disheartening. It transpired that Amina had not gone to Islamabad at all. All along she stayed in Lahore, having a gay time with her paramour. Aqueel almost went out of his mind on bearing this news. He had been confronted with a most horrible truth. He kept crying, "Amina, Amina!" while Amina, after killing her husband and showing another man the way to the gallows was now lying in the arms of a third lover. But this realisation had come to Aqueel too late when death was already knocking on his door. Sometimes he would wail loudly, at others, laugh and then flail the air with his fists and start raving.

At six after the roll-call one could still hear his cries emanating from his cell and would continue till the morning. At four the guards dragged him towards the well of death and his raving stopped only when the plank was dragged from under his feet.

In the morning when Amina did not turn up to claim his dead body word was sent to her to come to the jail. She flew at the messenger. "He means nothing to me," she said, "that I should take the responsibility of burying him. He is the murderer of my husband and has paid for his evil deed with death. I've nothing to do with him."

At last the jail authorities buried Aqeel's body at government expense. It is truly said that even God cannot delve into a man's fate and a woman's mind.

Driver Mohammed Azam

While we were there, driver Mohammed Azam was
languishing in a death cell of the Kot Lakhpat Jail,
awaiting his execution. A soldier in the army, he had been serving
as the driver of a Major at Lahore Cantonment. The Major's
wife, as it happened, was having an affair with her husband's
batman. Mohammed Azam was in the know of this fact but
he had all along kept discreetly silent over it. He knew that the
Major would be reluctant to believe him and the Begum, to
wreak vengeance on him, could create trouble for him.

One night, at about twelve, he drove the Major home from
the club, dead drunk. The Major asked him to stay in his kothi
for the night to which he agreed.

At about two he saw a shadow going towards the batman's
quarter. It took him no time to recognise the person; it was
none other than the Major's Begum. As luck would have it,
the Major woke up after half an hour. Not finding his wife in
her bed, he picked up his gun as a matter of habit and went
out to took for her. Probably he had already some suspicion in

his mind, for Azam saw the Major going towards the batman's quarter on stealthy steps. As he flung open the door of the batman's room he saw his Begum lying in the batman's arms. Both of them were lying stark naked. The Begum had not even thought in her dreams that her husband, whom she had left in bed dead drunk, would wake up so soon. Besides himself with rage, the Major pumped two bullets into the batman's body.

And then he realised what he had done. The batman was not yet dead, his pulse was still there. To save his skin, the Major immediately called the driver and pushing the batman into the back seat of the car asked the driver to proceed to the hospital. Having reached the hospital, they were just taking the batman out of the car when he breathed his last. The Major's face lost it colour.

Major acted fast. "The deed is done," he said to driver. "I had the better take the dead body with me and report the matter at the police station. Maybe, considering the circumstances the court may take a at the police lenient view of the case. If I abscond it will only make my case worse."

Acting on his master's advice, Azam turned the car engine towards the police station. Asking Azam to wait outside, the Major went into the police station and came out after half an hour accompanied by the Thana Incharge and two constables. The constables removed the dead man's body from the car and carried it in. The Thana Incharge asked Azam to come in for they wanted to record his statement. "Please report back at the Police Station with your Begum," the Thana Inchargesaid to the Major. "In the meanwhile I'll record your driver's statement."

Azam, a simple Pathan, had no idea what trick fate was going to play with him.

"You fool, what have you done?" the Thana Incharge barked at Azam as he was bustled into the officer's room. "It's just not done -killing a fellow soldier at the slightest altercation!"

"What are you saying, Thanedar Saheb?" Azam looked at the Thana Incharge aghast. "I had no argument with the batman. It's the Major Sabeb who had shot him dead. He had found his wife in bed with the batman."

"You son of a swine! Stop talking rot. Don't you feel ashamed of maligning your officer? If he had committed the murder he would not have spared an important eyewitness like you. Not would he have come to the police station with the dead body. His Begum will soon be here. She will clarify everything."

The innocent Azam started sobbing. He tried to convince the officer that be was innocent but the officer was in no mood to listen. He was pushed into the lock-up. A few minutes later the Major arrived with his wife. On the way he had tutored her as to what statement she was to make.

The Begum's statement was as follows:

"The batman Sadaq and the driver Azam have been in our

service for the past one year. Sadaq was a Sunni Musalman and Azam is a Shia Pathan. They often fell out. I reprimanded them frequently but they wouldn't stop squabbling. Today afternoon the batman said to the driver jokingly, "Azam, the Muharram is just round the corner. The days of your mourning have arrived."

At this Azam flew at him. "Hold your tongue, you son of a swine!" he said. "Otherwise, I'll put a bullet into your body and then it will be your mother and sisters who will be mourning for you." Highly provoked, both of them were locked in a fight. They threatened to kill each other and it was with great difficulty that I could separate them. But I could never believe that Azam would make his threat a reality. Tonight when Azam drove Major Saheb home the batman was away at a late night show. So Major Sabeb asked Azam to spend the night in the outer room and also gave him a gun to guard the house. After that I went to sleep.

"At about two-thirty I heard two gunshots being fired simultaneously. And then the screams of the batman. I and Major Saheb ran out of our house and found the batman lying in bed struggling for life. Azam was standing over him, gun in hand. We were still watching when he fired again and this time the bullet hit the batman's arm. Then Major Saheb ran up and snatched away the gun from him. The batman was still alive. Major Saheb put him in the car and took him to the hospital. But just now Major Sabeb told me that the batman died on the way to the hospital and that I was required at the police station to record my statement. And now I'm here recording my statement. I know nothing beyond what I have recorded."

After that the Thana Incharge recorded the Major's statement and lastly asked Azam to record his. The poor fellow stated the facts as he knew them but the Thana Incharge picked many holes in his statement and charged him under section 302 for murder.

His case came up before the Martial Law Court where he could not hold his ground against the Major's and his wife's statements. The case was over in three months. Azam was awarded capital punishment and sent to the Kot Lakhpat Jail to await his end.

Azam petitioned to the President for mercy but his request was turned down. Within twenty days of his coming to jail he received orders for his execution. He was the only child of widowed mother. She went wailing to the President and again begged for mercy for his son. The President gave her a *laddu*. "Here, mother, take this *laddu*. I've revoked your son's punishment. Orders have already gone out to the jail authorities not to hang your son. The telegram should reach them before you. Go in peace. Tomorrow your son will be with you."

But no such telegram reached the Kot Lakhpat Jail. Next morning when the mother reached the jail, beaming to meet her son, the jail authorities handed her her son's dead body. She fell down in a swoon, never to rise again. That day two

183

biers passed out together through the jail gate.

Many such biers are carried in the land of Martial Law. For years together this nation has been carrying the burden of Martial Law on its innocent shoulders. Only one messiah appeared on its horizon. Zulfikar Ali Bhutto. But as the history would record it, he was also hanged by the army.

It appears democracy has been strangled for ever in Pakistan. If a country's military wing, posing as a saviour of its people starts sucking their blood like wolves, the country finds itself at the end of its tether. It is no longer capable of working out its own salvation. Under such circumstances it is not unnatural for it to look to some outside power to set its house in order.

Warden Rafiq Shah

Rafiq Shah was the warden of the death cells of the Kot Lakbpat Jail. He kept a special eye on the pockets and tins of the new entrants. He wouldn't even forego a bribe of fifty paisa. He had two buffaloes in his house who were fed on the jail's *rotis* and gram. He would induce the prisoners to ask for an extra *roti* each which they would collect and pass on in one lot to the warden in the evening.

He managed to collect in this manner, going by two meals a day, 160 *Tons* from 80 prisoners. Two *Tons* weighed about 6 1/2 *chattacks*. Thus it added upto 50 kilo *Tons* and 10 kilo grams for his buffaloes. Some people even maintained that no food was cooked in Rafiq Shah's house; even his family subsisted on the jail food. In addition the prisoners also parted with their quotas of mustard oil, gur and soap in his favour. The rich prisoners often received fruits, sweets, ghee and toilet soap from home through the visitors, parts of which they regularly gifted away to Rafiq Shah.

The prisoners had their own fads. There were some who

were addicted to opium and there were others who were fond of *charas*. There were still others who wanted to have wine and women. In lieu of certain considerations Rafiq Shah satisfied all their wants. The most surprising part of the whole thing was that even while in the jaws of death the prisoners passionately gave in to such indulgences. Sometimes prostitutes came in posing as female relatives. This was within the knowledge of Rafiq Shah. But since they have great respect for purdah in Pakistan nobody would intrude into the privacy of these prisoners when burqa-clad women came to meet them. Supposedly relatives these women in burqa were actually from Tibbi or Shahi Mohalla, the red-light districts of Lahore. The prisoners were happy and so was Rafiq Shah and most of all Allah Mian who, sitting in his Heaven, watched these people enjoying without any fear of death or Allah himself.

But when this practice became too common even the bonafide relatives of prisoners became suspects. They were greeted with jeers and catcalls leading to unpleasantness among the prisoners and even would start skirmishes. Once this naked dance of sensuality was in full swing in the barrack of the condemned prisoners when some fun-loving prisoner reported the matter to a jail official. The barrack was raided. Many escaped but one was caught red-handed.

This landed Rafiq Shah in trouble. But he got away by saying that his job was only to escort the female visiting relatives upto the barracks. He could not scrutinise them due to the purdah which bad perforce to be respected. He had no way of knowing that the woman was not what she had declared herself to be. It was forbidden by Islam to look at another woman's face.

In the face of such argument, the Deputy Superintendent who was looking into this matter could do nothing but express his displeasure. Since no action could be taken against Rafiq Shah the practice continued unabated. Only the prisoners became more cautious.

On the eve of a prisoner's execution, Rafiq Shah would surreptitiously take away the prisoner's belongings such as his costly clothes, jersey, sweater, muffler and the like. When a rich prisoner was due for execution Rafiq Shah would start casting covetous looks on his things. "Son, hurry up!" he would say. "It's time for you to mount the gallows. Your things will be safe in my hands. They will find their way into my house. Since the prisoner's relatives were more anxious to claim his dead body than to sort out his belongings the situation generally worked to Rafiq's advantage.

Of course, Rafiq Shah put forward his rationale for what he did. As I had observed, in Pakistan cost of living was going up day by day. When I first started infiltrating into Pakistan food was quite cheap. At an eating place one could have his fill for four annas. One could buy a big nan for two annas which in Indian currency was equivalent to 12 paisas. It weighed about 150 grams or three chattacks. With the *nan* one would get a free helping of *daal*. A man could not eat more than two or at the most three *wins*. In the Anarkali Bazaar a man prepared maize and millet *rotis* which he sold at eight annas per *roti*, a sizable quantity of butter going free with it. He had with him a huge jar of *lassi* of which you could take as much as you liked for free. By the roadside they sold *halwa* from huge platters at the rate of three rupees per seer. The *halwa* contained almonds and pistachio and the smell wafting from it drew the attention of the people strolling through the bazaar. Squashes made from oranges and kinnu juices sold at eight annas per bottle and almond kernel at Rs. 10 per seer. A new fruit, kinnu, a hybrid from oranges and blood-red *maltas* sold at 20 pieces for a rupee. In fact there was no need to go in for a regular meal. One could easily manage to live on fruits and they were good for health. A cup of tea cost two annas.

The salary scales were also fixed commensurate with the living conditions. A police constable drew a salary of Rs. 70 per month whereas his counterpart in India got Rs. 225 per month. In India a police inspector who was paid Rs. 700 per month rode on a ramshackle bicycle while a Pakistani police inspector who earned Rs. 350 per month drove home in a car. Only city boys and girls were fashion-conscious. Till then the villagers were mostly immune to it. Tight clothes were in vogue those days which in Lahore went by the name of paddy-fashion.

In Pakistan even the daily necessities of life were imported. Articles ranging from needles to foreign watches, TV sets and cameras were quite cheap. In India the price of gold was pegged at Rs.210 per tola whereas in Pakistan it cost only Rs. 90 per tola. Gold imported from the Gulf countries was smuggled out to India. Foreigners swarmed the country and were a common sight on the highways of Pakistan, most of them hitch-hikers. There was a glut of Chinese goods and Chinese literature.

In mills and factories labour unions were just trying to find their feet. Now the rudderless had at least found their direction and there were already murmurs of protest against the army rule symbolised by General Ayub. An opposition party in the real sense of the word had just come into being and had started making its presence felt in all the four states constituting Pakistan. All the newspapers of Pakistan such as Imroz, Nawai-Waqt and the Dawn were in sympathy with this movement. To resist more influence on people censorship had been imposed on the press. Despite that people were joining the People's Party in large numbers. If there was any one who enjoyed the people's affection more than the Qaid-e-Azam Mohammed Ali Jinnah it was none other than Qaid-e-Awam, Janab Zulfikar Ali Bhutto.

People swarmed in thousands just to have a glimpse of Bhutto. They were prepared to die for him at a mere nod of his head. People were flogged at road crossings, the workers of the People's Party were called at the police stations and beaten indiscriminately, false cases were started against them and their women humiliated. But it was now beyond the means of the tottering military regime to stem the flood. Every day there were bomb blasts in one city or the other and government buildings were set on fire. The People's Party was even prepared for guerrilla warfare to gain its ends.

Political meetings predominantly attended by young students would continue late into the night. Bhutto had inflamed the passions of the impressionable youth to such an extent that neither Ayub nor Yahya Khan had been able to curb their zeal. It was Pakistan's misfortune that Bhutto Saheb became complacent and Zia-ul-Haq turned the tables on him. The conspiracy that was hatched against him in 1972-73 led to the arrest of 129 army officers. But Bhutto failed to attach any significance to this tell-tale warning. How Zia-ul-Haq came to power and how Bhutto was hanged will be narrated in subsequent pages.

Every Pakistani family tried to impress upon others that meat forms a dish at its every meal. Even a small piece of meat in a pot of vegetables has to be there. To eat *daal is* considered to be a sign of poverty.

Though the majority of the populace have changed their religion yet Hinduism is still ingrained in their blood. They fly kites on the day of Basant, the Spring festival of the Hindus. There is public illumination to celebrate the day when the Prophet had his *nikah* and the day on which he became one with Allah. Crackers are also burst on these days.

On weddings *mehndi* (myrtle) is applied to the bride's palms

190

and feet. Bridal songs are sung and the dowry given on behalf of the bride. The bride sheds tears while parting from her parents and coins are showered over the bridal palanquin and crackers burst. Even at death more or less similar rites are observed except that the Hindus cremate the dead while the Muslims bury them. A community prayer is held to ask for peace for the soul of the dear departed. In India the Brahmins are fed while among Muslims the maulvis are invited to the feast. When I take stock of all these, I recollect what our late minister Janab Mohammed Karim Bhai Chagla said in 1965. He had reiterated that in our Indo-Pak subcontinent the forefathers of all the Muslims were Hindus. The Hindu blood still flowed in their veins. By changing the label of religion the blood ties could not be broken.

If all this is true which is borne out by what I observe around me then why do these walls of hatred rise between us? In Pakistan people enthusiastically listen to the request songs broadcast by the All-India Radio. Even today they love to hear the programme of Urdu Majlis and the songs of Rafi keep them spellbound. Lata's songs are on every Pakistani child's tips.

In our own country we rave over Nurjahan's and Mehdi Hasan's ghazals. We read Faiz Ahmed Faiz with great interest. Janab Josh Malihabadi who had migrated to Pakistan in a huff lived to regret his decision. In one of his verses he says, let us hug each other and ask where is the enemy.

People on both sides of the border are anxious to unite with one another. They want to demolish the walls which they had erected between them in a frenzy of madness. Only the political leaders on both sides stand in the way; they are chary of the people on both sides coming together. If the people are united what will happen to their political careers? And if we don't fight with each other the foreign powers would lose the very lucrative market for the sale of their arms. Will not the staggering expenditure on armaments adversely affect the economy of a small country like Pakistan? Both the countries go in for armaments on a point of national prestige though they claim that they are doing it out of a sense of security.

While I was in Pakistan no significant nation-building work was in evidence. The old landmarks were still there in Lahore. For instance, the Dayal Singh College and Library and the Gulab Devi Hospital was still working efficiently, when DAV High School and College were converted into Islamic institutions. And that all for their kind of advancement.

The villages in Pakistan are in bad shape and most of them are still without electricity. The Pakistani rulers are not paying much heed to this aspect of national development. Their efforts are mostly directed towards instigating the Pakistanis against India. They want to divert their people's minds from the rampant exploitation by the vested interests by raising the bogey of -India. Whenever the rulers find that their government is in danger of being overthrown they raise such cries as 'Kashmir belongs to Pakistan!' Ayub adopted this strategy and so did Yahya Khan and it is quite probable that the ruler who would follow them would not go far from such activities. Both sides have regretted the futility of the 1965 war, which was not of India's making. But Pakistan has not allowed its hatred die.

Instead it fanned the flames of hatred only to generate reciprocal feelings. Every year on the 6th of September Pakistani flags dipped in blood are flown over all big cities of Pakistan. Every ruler and every mullah of Pakistan raises the cry of the Indian wolf being on the rampage against Pakistan. This helps the rulers and the powers that be to skim off the cream for themselves. That is why every ruler of Pakistan talks less about national reconstruction and more about the regeneration of Islam. Though living in the twentieth century, the rulers would like to keep the people in – the sixteenth century.

Turmoil in Bangladesh

The daily public demonstrations and hartals were getting too much for Yahya Khan and be was at last driven to holding General Elections. At that time Bhutto Saheb's People's Party was in ascendancy in West Pakistan and Sheikh Mujib-ur-Rahman's Awami League in East Pakistan. There were other political parties too. For instance, there were Air Marshal Asghar Khan's Party and Maulana Maududi's Jamiat-e-Islam. But they did not count for much. It was the general belief that only Bhutto's and Sheikh Mujib's parties could deliver the goods.

Though General Yahya Khan had announced about the holding of General Elections he was in no mood to let political power slip out of his hands. He cunningly created conditions to prevent the People's Party and the Awami League front joining hands to assume power. In one of his public speeches Bhutto had alluded to Mujib and said: "You rule there and I'll rule here." To forestall such a move Yahya Khan's followers had organised demonstrations against Bhutto, bringing him a bad name. It was said that Bhutto's design was to create a serious rift between the two wings of Pakistan leading to the division of the country so that he could hold full sway over one part.

On the other hand Sheikh Mujib-ur-Rahman, who was popularly known as Banga Bandhu had formulated a seven-point programme for the people of East Pakistan. For years he had watched the Bengalis being regarded as second class citizens by the West Pakistanis who had sucked the Bengalis white and thrived. East Pakistan was the repository of valuable exchange carriers such as jute, tea and natural gas. It accounted for 70 per cent of the foreign exchange earned by Pakistan. And yet it was West Pakistan which reaped the benefit; the people of East Pakistan lived in penury.

Yahya Khan and Bhutto hatched a conspiracy to deprive Mujib of his political right to rule. Yahya Khan made a trip to East Pakistan with the avowed purpose of discussing the Seven-Point Programme with Mujib. Mujib had no inkling of the game that was going to be played with him. His house was ransacked by the soldiers, many of his followers were killed and he was himself put under arrest and taken to West Pakistan.

This subterfuge of the Pakistani army infuriated the Bengalis of East Pakistan, throwing the whole country in turmoil. Political demonstrations and hartals became the order of the day. In desperation, the Pakistani army started genocide of unarmed Bengalis among whom the Hindus were specially singled out for slaughter. The army stationed tanks outside the Dacca University and fixed guns in the university hostels. Imagination boggled at the brutality exhibited in their slaughter.

The soldiers entered the college hostels and raped the girls en masse. Unable to bear such fiendish treatment many girls died on the spot. The soldiers cut the girls' breasts and impaled them on their bayonets. So much so that even girls of ten were not spared. Now the Bengalis had only two ways open to them – either they should wear the chains of slavery and lick the shoes of the West Pakistanis for ever or they should tie shrouds round their heads and take to the war-path.

They could not face the Pakistani army in East Bengal in an open conflict and hence they took to guerrilla warfare. The Pakistani army not being conversant with the topography of East Bengal was always taken by surprise; it did not know when and from which direction the attack would be coming. The Bengalis would emerge from nowhere, do the damage and disappear.

The East Pakistani police had also rebelled. The police rifles and the guns of the Bengali regiments were pointed at the Pakistani army.

As misfortune would have it, two Kashmiri Muslims – Mohammed Ashraf and Hashim Qureshi by name who were striving for Kashmir's separation from India hijacked an Indian plane to Pakistan.

The Indian government retaliated by banning the flights of Pakistani aircrafts over the Indian territory. The government also prohibited the movement of Pakistani ships through Indian waters.

As a result, the Pakistani army in East Pakistan was cut off and bottled up like a rat in a trap.

The besieged army could not be rushed reinforcements and arms from the West. Driven against the wall, it indulged in wanton butchery of civil population. Its savagery increased as the days passed and at one stage it was feared that the Bengalis may be wiped out of existence. But as later developments showed this silence on the part of the Bengalis was only a lull before the storm which burst upon East Pakistan in December 1971 in the form of a war.

The effect of the turmoil in Bangladesh also percolated to the Indian prisoners in the Pakistani jails. Most of the people held us in contempt and there were many who hated the very sight of us. If they chanced upon a stray Indian prisoner in the jail they went at him full tilt.

I recall one Shah Mohammed, a police inspector, lodged in one of the death cells who had been awarded capital punishment. Before the Bangladesh war started he was very friendly with me but as the situation in Bangladesh worsened his attitude towards me started changing gradually. One afternoon as I was passing by his cell tie called me. "Pandit, come here. I'll give you a cigarette." As I approached him, not suspecting any mischief, he extended his hand through the iron grill and gripped my throat. "You dirty Indian day, I'm going to kill you!" he cried. "I'm already condemned to death and one more death will not make any difference in my punishment. Rather by killing a *kafir* I'll attain martyrdom." He tried him to throttle me. I did not know from where that sixty-five year old man gathered so much strength. I managed to scream which brought the warden and a nambardar rushing to the scene. The nambardar stuck the man on his head which loosened his grip over my throat, If an old and educated man of some status can behave in this barbarous manner one can well imagine how the illiterate and rustic Pakistani prisoners would have reacted to the situation.

After this episode I did not venture out of my cell for many days. The Jail Superintendent had also issued instructions that when the Pakistani prisoners were let out of their barracks the Indian prisoners should be kept confined to theirs so as to be out of their reach. The Indian prisoners were also prohibited from going to other barracks. Not only the Pakistani prisoners, even the attitude of the jail officers had changed. The Indian prisoners were beaten over trifles, their fatigue duty was intensified and they were made to work like animals. Luckily, the practice of grinding corn and crushing oil for which prisoners were drafted like animals had been abolished in jails by law. Left to themselves the jail officers would have gladly drafted the Indian prisoners to do these back-breaking jobs.

I stopped going to my Pakistani friends even when they invited I discerned that the attitude of all of them had changed without a single exception. A miasma seemed to be hanging in the air and we had to breathe in that killing atmosphere. It was the same hatred which I had seen in my childhood between the Hindus and Muslims in 1947 at the time of the partition of the country. The thought where all this was going to end was causing me deep concern. My case had not even started. I worried and worried over what kind of punishment would be awarded to me and for how many more years those eyes full of hate would keep throwing their darts in my face.

My Trial Begins

The day I had long since been awaiting at last arrived. I was informed that my summary court martial would be held in the Shahi Qila of Lahore. This news caused me great apprehension. As I could see my trial was being held at an interrogation centre where the police held full sway and could influence the witnesses and manipulate their statements to suit their end. The police could also ask a person of their choice to identify the accused and openly tutor him to make an incriminating statement.

The chairman of the summary court martial was a Major, rather young for his years. He was a Syyed by caste and whenever I tried to have my say in the course of the proceedings he would try to intimidate me into silence by glaring at me; it appeared as if he was going to gobble me up.

On the first day of my trial they kept me waiting the whole day and sent me back without conducting any business. I was told that the chairman of the summary court martial had failed to turn up. In fact it was a clever ruse by the police to give their witnesses time to have a good look at me to ensure that they did not make any mistake in identifying me.

The next day too the Major did not show up till twelve. In his absence, Janab Mohammed Azim Durrani, the DSP of the Shahi Qila, called me in his office. Syyed Mirza Javed Dastgir, a first class magistrate was also present in his room. It immediately occurred to me that he would also depose in my case. Durrani Saheb sent for tea and offered it to both of us.

"Didn't I tell you Bhaskar?" Durrani said to me. "But you did not care to listen and here you're involved in this rigmarole of court martial. You can even be awarded capital punishment. Even if you escape death you will rot in Pakistani jails till you meet your end. Yes, even at the expiry of your term you'll be interned here. Now all that will fall to your lot will be jail *rotis* and a canister of kerosene to burn your dead body. Your parents may not even get your ashes because these wretched Indian High Commission people do not come to claim the ashes of the Indian prisoners."

He cast a hard look and continued: "If you had agreed to my proposal and given word that you would work for Pakistan we would have declared you an escapee from jail and given this fact wide publicity through the papers, radio and TV. You would have come a hero in the eyes of your countrymen and you could have done counter-espionage for us without arousing any suspicion."

Durrani put me on my guard and I did not want to make

any mistake about it.

"Durrani Saheb, you are again talking like a child," I said. "Do you think the Indian Intelligence is so stupid as to believe in the canard of my escaping from a Pakistani Jail? Not one of the Indian prisoners languishing in Pakistani jails since 1950 has been able to escape till now. Am I a superman that they would believe that I could do it? And where is the guarantee that the drama you wish to enact would only relate to my escape? It could as well lead to my annihilation. As for imposing the death sentence on me I see no valid ground for it. After an intensive and gruelling investigation lasting over two and a half years you have not been able to establish my link with any Pakistani. Nor have you been able to recover from me any such incriminating document as a paper, a map or a photograph which could prove that I've been spying in Pakistan. At the most only my circumcision goes against me. If you punish me with death just on that account you will be exposing your law to ridicule, because after passing the sentence on me you will be required to send a copy of the judgment to the Indian High Commission. No court worth its name would award me death sentence on the mere surmise that I could be a spy. As for Samund Singh's evidence, he is now a prisoner of the government of Pakistan. I would maintain that he has deposed against me on the allurement of being released from jail."

"Son, don't try to fly so high," Durrani said. "I can clip your wings anytime. You must know our rulers, don't believe in sentiments. The day your judgement is pronounced You'll forget all niceties of law.

I said, "It's the most surprising dispensation of law that the police knows in advance that I'm going to be awarded death sentence. If such is the case then why this mockery of justice? Why this play-acting? Put end of this farce. Send me to the gallows."

Durrani smiled. "Son, some dramas are very necessary," he said. "Life itself is a big drama. Well, you act your role and we shall act ours. But I really feel sorry for an educated and handsome youth like you."

We were still talking when a youngman is plain clothes entered Durrani's room. "Come, Sayyed Dilshad Hussain," Durrani welcomed him. Then he turned to me. "Bhaskar, you know him, of course," he said. "You used to stay in his Grand Hotel at Gujranwala."

I was taken by surprise. I had never seen this man before. "Chaudhri Saheb, keep the play going. After an hour you could as well produce a girl and say that she is my wife with whom I've been spending my nights."

My jibe hurt Durrani. "My boy, you're trying to be impertinent while I'm treating you with extreme courtesy. No Pakistani woman can be so depraved as to claim you as her husband."

I realised that it was leading us nowhere and I decided to bold my peace.

A soldier came and announced that the Chairman of the Summary Court Martial had arrived. Then the drama started. Every witness reeled out his statement parrot-like. Syyed Dilshad Hussain, the manager of Grand Hotel, Gujranwala was also there. I was surprised when he took his oath by touching the Quran and then proceeded to record his statement. After that one Bhagdin, a resident of village Sabiwal took an oath and made a statement against me. More witnesses came whom I watched as a spectator.

When magistrate Syyed Mirza Javed Dastgir got down to recording his statement I interrupted him and asked him, "Pir Saheb, will you be good enough to tell the court that when you were taking down my statement whether Raja Gul-Anar Khan was inside your chamber or outside it?"

"Outside the chamber," he replied.

"Are you sure? Mind you, you are saying all this on oath. What you have said could be a lie."

The Chairman of the Summary Court Martial blew up at my remark.

"You must behave yourself," he said. "You've got the answer to your question and that's enough. Next time you'll not be allowed to pass any strictures at my witnesses. Understand!"

Now I could do nothing about it except keeping quiet. I did not cross-examine any other witness. When Raja Gul-Anar Khan's turn came he dictated his statement and then turned to me. "Bhaskar, have you anything to ask?"

I said, "Raja Saheb, if I say anything it may be construed as contempt of court. Therefore, I do not want to add to my crimes. If the rule in this court is to keep one's mouth shut then there is no point in uttering anything. It'll not only be futile but foolish too. Even so, if the court permits I would like to know that when I was making my statement before magistrate Syyed Mirza Javed Dastgir whether you were in his chamber or outside it?"

"I was neither inside nor outside. I was standing in the door."

"Could you tell me how far was the door from the Magistrate's chair? Could you hear my statement or not?"

He replied, "As far as I remember I was about three or four feet away from both of you and I could distinctly hear what you were saying."

"'Thank you very much, Saheb. I've nothing more to ask."

It was a very important legal point. According to the law when an accused's statement is being recorded under Section 164 it is incumbent upon the recording officer that no one else should be present in the room except the accused and the magistrate. So much so that even the police has to stay outside and out of earshot. Now that Raja Saheb had given the reply to my satisfaction, the Chairman of the Summary Court Martial squirmed in his chair.

"He's a clever fellow, Raja Saheb," he said. "He has caught you on the wrong fool."

"I understand every thing, Major Saheb," Raja Saheb replied.

"But I can't help it. I'm speaking on oath. I can't tell a lie. I did not want to remain in the chamber at that time but I had orders from the high-ups and I had to obey."

On hearing this the Major knitted his brows. "Have you anything to say in your defence?" he asked.

I replied, "As for my statement is concerned I've only to add that it is legally indefensible to hold a summary court martial in the premises of the police headquarters of the Interrogation Center in the Shahi Qila and as such this court itself has no legal standing. It is therefore meaningless to make any statement before such a court. Hence I reserve my statement for the time being. Whatever I have to say I'll say it before the Field General Court Martial."

The Major exploded and said, "Who do you think you are? You have been chattering for a long time. It appears the fear of punishment has put you out of your mind. If I want I can right now have you flogged for contempt of court. But I must have pity on a man doomed to death. After hearing the statement of all the witnesses I have come to the conclusion that you are a great danger to the security of our country. Hence I recommend death sentence for you and I would like to see how the Field General Court Martial absolves you of this charge."

"Thank you, Major Saheb," I replied. "I never expected anything better from you. You couldn't have done worse, anyway. As for losing my senses for fear of punishment you must know that those who cross the border under the shadow of bayonets never fear death. I'll get what is ordained for me. But why should you embitter your tongue? An incumbent of the President's court need not be so gruff nor does the law permit it."

He was incensed at my remark but before he could speak I said Khuda Hafiz and proceeded towards the door. The soldiers handcuffed me and I started climbing down the stairs, jingling the chains on my feet. Raja Saheb was standing below in the fort. I asked he if he would permit me to stop for a minute at the Gurudwara of Guru Arjan Dev where the Guru had attained his martyrdom. He said that the law did not allow it but he graciously acceded to my request. I had no words to express my gratitude, particularly for the favour he had done me by speaking the truth in the court.

He left after the giving necessary instructions to the guards and I kept watching with tear-dimmed eyes the man who was notoriously known as the 'Butcher' of the fort.

Guru Arjan Dev's garudwara is just in front of the Shahi Qila and it was now being renovated. % As we stepped into the vestibule the guard removed my handcuffs. But my feet were still shackled and I entered the gurudwara to the jingling of my chains. This is the place where they had killed the Guru by pouring burning sand over his head. I had a rupee in my pocket which I had borrowed from a Pakistani prisoner before leaving for the Shahi Qila. I kneeled in memory of the great

Guru and the following lines of Guru Govind Singh rang in my ears:

When you are with me there is no fear in my heart

I have your benediction,

You are my protection.

I am one with you.

I felt inspired as if some divine power was surging through me. The fear of punishment had vanished from my mind. I was brought back to the Kot Lakhpat jail in a tonga and I wrote to my parents at home that a case would soon be started against me and that they should pray for me. I made no reference to the Summary Court Martial and about the possibility of death sentence which was now looming large before me. I did not want to add to my parents' worries. But as I learnt later this news had already reached them over the radio and through newspaper reports. They were under the impression that orders had already been passed for my execution. My mind boggles at the thought as to how my aged parents and my wife would have taken the news.

Field General Court Martial

A month later I was told one morning that I was scheduled to appear before the Field General Court Martial. A Colonel and four Majors constitute the Court as such in which the Colonel acts as the presiding officer.

A Major acts as an advocate on behalf of the prosecution while another Major pleads on behalf of the defendant.

When Col. Rashid, the presiding officer, informed me that whatever I had to tell to the court would only be conveyed through my advocate I raised an objection. "I don't require any legal assistance," I said. "I'll plead my own case."

The Colonel replied that in conformity with the legal procedure it was incumbent on me to have an advocate to plead my case. "If you don't agree to it you must give in writing that you will yourself cross-examine the witnesses and argue your case."

In deference to his wishes I gave it in writing. After that the entire bench stood up and took an oath by touching the Quran that they would do full justice to the accused and that if a witness' statement was suspect they would go by the voice of their own conscience. After that the advocate on behalf of the prosecution took the oath that he would fight the case with rectitude keeping the best interests of his country in view and would make no effort to falsely implicate the accused. Then it was the turn of the defence advocate to take his oath to the effect that he would do his best to safeguard the interests of the accused. I also took the oath that I'll speak the truth and nothing but the truth. The proceedings started.

Naib Subedar Mohammed Aslam of the 596 FIU, Lahore was the first prosecution witness. When I tried to cross-examine him he objected saying that I had no business to put him any questions. At this the Colonel flared up. "Who are you to object when we are giving the accused the right to put up questions?" he asked. "Answer his questions truly and honestly."

I asked the witness if he had found any papers, camera or a wireless set in my possession at the time of my arrest which could arouse his suspicion that I was acting as a spy.

"No," he replied.

"During the course of your investigation did you find that I had any link with any Pakistani citizen?"

He again replied in the negative.

I told the court that I had no more questions to ask the witness.

The prosecution presented its second witness – Syyed

Dilshad Hussain, Manager, Grand Hotel, Gujranwala.

He said in his statement: "About three years ago this man came to my hotel in the evening along with three companions. They told their names respectively as Mohammed Aslam, Imamuddin and Abdul Rahman. They said that they were residents of Chak 7, Sahiwal, Montgomery, and that the following morning they would be taking the old man Imamuddin to Daska for the treatment of his eyes. Accordingly, I recorded their names in my register and gave them charpoys for the night. Most probably they stayed in my hotel for three days. They would go out in the morning and return at night. After his arrest, taking the cue from his own statement the police sent for me asking me to appear before the police with the register in which their names have been recorded."

As soon as he had finished his statement I asked him, "Syyed Dilshad Hussain, you say that you have written these names in your register. Can you once again jot down these names on a plain piece of paper?"

"Why not?" he said and scribbled the names on a sheet of paper.

I handed the sheet of paper to Colonel Khursheed. "Sir, kindly have a look at this sheet of paper," I said. "Does this handwriting tally with that in the register?"

The court carefully examined both the handwritings. "Yes, they tally more or less," the Colonel said.

"Hazoor, it's not a question of more or less. Your honour

has taken the oath that you will do justice to my case. You may kindly call a handwriting expert and defer further hearing till his opinion had been obtained."

"All right," the Colonel replied and instantly called for a handwriting expert on phone who arrived within fifteen minutes.

"No, Janab, there's a world of difference between the two handwritings," the expert said after carefully scrutinising the two handwritings.

The Colonel glared at Dilshad Hussain. "You son of a pimp," he growled at him. "You're a Syyed and you have taken an oath on the Quran and yet you speak lies. What harm has this foreigner done you? He can be hanged on the basis of your statement. I award you ten lashes and six months imprisonment for misleading the court."

Dilshad Hussain started crying and begged for mercy but the military police pushed him out of the court and led him away crying.

After that Syyed Mirza Javed Dastgir recorded his statement. I put him the same question that I had asked him at the summary court martial. He again gave the same answer.

Next came Raja Gul-Anar Khan and he admitted that when I was recording my statement he was present in Mirza Javed Dastgir's chamber.

As I have already stated it is a point of law that when an accused is making his confessional statement under Section

164, nobody other than the accused and the magistrate should be present in the chamber. Otherwise it would be taken that the accused had made his statement under duress and such statements are not taken into account by the court.

The next witness was the sixty-five year old Bhagdin of Chak No. 7, Sahiwal, Montgomery who said, "This had happened about three years ago. The accused Mohan Lal Bhaskar alias Mohammed Aslam came to me at about seven one evening. Samund Singh alias Imamuddin and a young man, Abdul Rahman were with him. I knew Imamuddin and hence I fed them and gave them shelter for the night. They said that they had to catch the morning bus for Multan. I gave them breakfast in the morning and bade them farewell. I have no knowledge where they went after that. This man had never visited me before. Nor did he meet me subsequently."

Six months ago this man Bhagdin had deposed against Samund Singh before the Field General Martial's court. His statement against Samund Singh was so long and involved that he had to appear before the court for two days. The Major who had now been assigned to my defence had occupied the bench at the Field General Court Martial in connection with the hearing of Samund Singh's case also. Bhagdin had appeared before him on two consecutive days.

I asked the old man: "Bhagdin, do you recognise Major Khalid who is my defence advocate and is now sitting by my side?"

"No," Bhagdin shook his head.

"Please have a close look," I said. "May be you have seen him before from very close quarters."

Bhagdin walked up and carefully looked at Major Khalid. "No, Janab," he again shook his head. "I've never seen him before."

"All right, Bhagdin, you may go. I've no more questions to ask."

I addressed the court: "This man Bhagdin who is now deposing against me had also been produced six months ago before my honourable defence advocate, Major Khalid, when he was a member of the bench of the Field General Court Martial in connection with the hearing of Samund Singh alias Imamuddin's case. This was barely six months ago. He has not been able to recognise Major Khalid whom he had seen six months ago continuously for two days but he claims to have recognised me although he had seen me three years back and that too for a short while at night. From this it is quite evident that he has been tutored by the police to depose against me. There is not an iota of truth in his statement."

The judges started whispering among themselves. I felt that my case was taking a turn in my favour. If the court dispensed justice in the real sense of the word there was not even a remote chance of my being awarded death sentence,

I was asked to make my statement. I stated: "I, Mohan Lal Bhaskar alias Mohammed Aslam, am a resident of Ferozpur. In 1968 I was employed as a school teacher at Government

High School at Atari in Amritsar district. This place being very close to the Wagah border I was sometimes fired by a desire to visit Pakistan. One day Samund Singh visited me to have a child admitted in the school. In the course of the talk he told me that he had many relations living across the Wagah border and he frequently visited them on the sly. I expressed my desire to visit Pakistan and asked him if he could help me in this regard. He said that it was not a problem for him and I crossed the border with him on the night of 16th September and spent the night in the fields near the border village of Hadian. In the morning we caught the bus to Lahore. In the bus Samund Singh happened to meet an acquaintance, Jamil by name. I did not know him. He took us to the Zamindara Hotel at Lahore where he gave Samund Singh some opium with his tea and left saying that he would be back soon. After he left we were put under arrest by the Pakistan Military Intelligence. I was kept under investigation for over two and a half years during which period I suffered constant harassment at the hands of the military and the police. But it could not produce any evidence to prove that I had been spying against Pakistan. As for my circumcision I did it on medical advice after marriage. I am absolutely innocent. Except crossing the border illegally I've committed no other offence. The maximum punishment for illegally crossing the border is six months. But I have already spent two and a three quarter years in Pakistani jails. Hence I would plead with the court that considering my circumstances I may be freed. Even so, if the Honourable court considers it necessary to punish me then I may be punished as per your law for crossing the border and I shall cheerfully accept your verdict."

The prosecution advocate banking on the hackneyed statements of the witnesses indicted me as an arch criminal and requested the court to award me maximum punishment which should serve as an objective lesson to other Indians not to dare undermine the security of Pakistan.

"All right, Bhaskar," Colonel Khursheed said, "We are sending you back to the jail. One of us will go there and apprise you of the verdict of the court."

Colonel Khursheed had returned to Pakistan only a few months back after the holocaust in Bangladesh. So I had a fear that he, being prejudiced, might take it out on me.

A week later I was in my cell when I was informed by a chit from the jail office that a military officer was there to see me. The nambardar took me to to the office. It was one of the Majors representing the judges of Field General Court Martial.

"Bhaskar, I've come to tell you about the court's decision," he said. With baited breath I waited for his next words.

He pronounced the verdict: "Mohan Lal Bhaskar alias Mohammed Aslam, son of Imamuddin, after hearing your case the court has come to the conclusion that your illegal entry into Pakistan and your movement in various places prove that you have been acting in a manner prejudicial to the interests of Pakistan and are a great risk to its security. You have also been involved in the crime of espionage. Therefore, under Section 3 of the Official Secrets Act read with 59 Pakistan Army Act the Court awards you fourteen years, rigorous imprisonment. If you so desire, you are permitted to file a mercy petition before the President."

Overjoyed, I ran like a mad man towards my barrack, leaving the nambardar far behind. My fellow prisoners, seeing me beaming, thought that I had been released.

"What's happened?" They asked.

"Ram Banbas," I replied. "Fourteen years exile."

"But you look so happy!" they said.

"Why, isn't it a cause for joy that I've escaped death?"

I informed my people at home that I had been awarded fourteen years imprisonment, adding that they should not worry over it. God willing, we may yet find a way of being together.

Lahore to Mianwali

I was spending better days in Lahore, happy over the fact that I had escaped death sentence. In East Bengal the situation was deteriorating day by day for Pakistanis. After a prisoner's case is decided, as is the common practice, he is transferred to some Central Jail. I was told that some such step was also being contemplated in my case and that they were in consultation with the higher authorities. There was a possibility of my being sent either to Multan Central Jail or to the one at Mianwali.

I started making preparations in anticipation of the transfer which I realised would not take long to materialise. When Achcha Pahalwan learnt about my impending transfer he visited me in my cell and gave me two hundred rupees in ten rupee notes. "Pandit, keep the money," he insisted, "You never know, it may come handy sometime."

For me those two hundred rupees were as good as two thousand rupees. Another Pakistani friend, Jamil, gave me fifty rupees. I also got some more gifts in terms of small amounts.

In this manner I was able to lay by a substantial amount, more than enough to meet unforeseen contingencies. This also raised my morale for the change.

The day arrived. The guard came to take me away – one havaldar and three constables. My chains were removed.

At seven-thirty we caught the Mari-Indus Express from Lahore. Achcha Pahalwan even wanted to give me a pistol so that I could threaten the guards on the way and stage an escape. But I declined the offer. I knew the guards would search me before we started on the journey and if the pistol was discovered Achcha Pahalwan would also be in trouble. "No, friend, now only Allah would show me the way," I told him.

Mari-Indus Express is not a fast train. Once I seriously thought of slipping the handcuffs from my wrists and jumping down from the running train but then I decided to leave everything to my fate. There was no point in acting in a reckless manner. The train reached Mianwali at nine next morning.

Mianwali is a hot place situated in a sandy region. The jail being about two and a half miles from the railway station the Havaldar hired a tonga. I sat in front between two constables and we started off to our destination where I was destined to spend the best part of my youth behind the jail's walls. The havaldar, asked the constables to keep a close watch on me – an unnecessary instruction for there was no chance of my escape.

"Havaldar Saheb, if I wanted to escape I could have found an opportunity for it during the long train journey," I said, a bit peeved.

"I didn't mean it that way," the Havaldar said. "You know we have to be careful. Last year we were bringing an Indian prisoner, Joginder, from the Montgomery Central Jail. He also hailed from your district and had been sentenced to fourteen years. On hearing the judgment he went out of mind and on returning to the jail tried to kill himself by cutting off his penis. Luckily, he survived after a protracted treatment. He had been transferred to the Mianwali Jail and like you he was also sitting in front between two constables. We got down on the road in front of the jail. A quiet and simple looking man, we never knew what he could be up to. As the constables led him towards the jail gate he fell headlong under a passing truck and was killed instantly. I was suspended from duty. If there had not been a previous record of attempted suicide against him I would have surely lost my job. I had to face great difficulty in getting myself reinstated. That's why I've to be careful. You have also been sentenced to fourteen years in jail."

"Yes, one can never be too careful, Havaldar Saheb," I said. "But I have no such intentions. I want to go back home solid and whole. My father, my mother, my wife and child are anxiously looking forward to my return."

"*Shabash!*" he gave a hearty pat on my back. "A man should

never lose heart. Only the brave suffer. Only the lion and bulbul are put in the cage. Have you ever seen a dog or a crow being caged? With luck, you may yet return to your country."

We passed through the jail gate. A casual glance at the exterior of the jail made my heart sink. The jail had *kuchcha* walls made of mud. From which one could guess the condition of the barracks. The Kot Lakhpat Jail at Lahore was made of solid bricks and had flush system latrines. Most surprising of all, the barracks had even taps and ceiling fans.

At Mianwali my only consolation was that I would be in the midst of my own countrymen, most of whom like me were undergoing long imprisonments.

They searched me in the vestibule. They could not find any money on my person for they could not even conceive where I could have hidden it. The Jail Superintendent was hard of hearing and I had to shout out my name and other details to him. I was lodged in barrack No. 2 where the Indian prisoners were kept. It was popularly known as the 'Sikh Compound'.

The Indian prisoners received me with open arms. They were surprised to find me in their midst for they thought I had been awarded death sentence. There were eighty Indian prisoners in this barrack, eight of them having gone insane on account of electric shocks and such other mental torture. It was agonising to see their matted hair, naked bodies and silly antics.

I was introduced to all the prisoners – those who had been incarcerated before me and those who found their way into the jail after me. Sadajit Singh from Ferozpur whom I had known since childhood was also among them. He was popularly known as 'Shilajeet'. From him I learnt at first hand about the condition of my family. We turned the occasion into a sort of get together and made it a celebration. The barrack had fifteen rooms, housing five to six prisoners each. Each room had a lunatic.

The inmates were divided in two categories – prisoners numbering thirty and internees, who were forty. The internees were not required to do any labour whereas the prisoners were put to hard labour. The only redeeming feature was that we were not taken out of the compound and the internees lent us a helping hand on the sly to help us complete our individual quotas of work. On the very next morning of my arrival a nambardar brought me ten seers of munj (long strips of softened bamboo) for me to make strings from it. I had to pound the stuff and make it into fine strings which requires a special technique which I did not know as I had never tried my hand at such jobs before. I was still puzzling over he matter when three internees came to my rescue. They got down to the job and finished it before twelve. They often helped me out in this manner.

I started going to the other barracks to widen my contacts. I would study the prisoners' palms and tell their future. They would reciprocate by making me gifts of gur, cigarettes and soap etc., which I shared with my friends. Since I had money I obtained four cartons of a good brand of cigarettes from the bazaar which I would sell to Pakistani prisoners at a premium. I utilized this profit in buying extra packets of cigarettes and distributing them free among my friends. Each carton yielded four or five packets.

Mianwali was a very hot place. The days were unbearably hot and the nights chilly. We suffered from prickly heat, the eruptions assuming the size of large pimples which turned our complexions dark. What irked me most was that I had stopped getting letters from home. The Deputy Superintendent nicknamed 'Mirza' was a mean fellow and he cast the letters of the Hindu prisoners to the flames for he could not brook the trouble of censoring them. Our letters reached India all right but without our getting any in return.

I had no reliable friend outside the jail at whose address I could get my letters. And then who would run the risk of handling the letters of a spy? It was just the beginning of my journey and I had to trudge a distance of fourteen long years. Besides, there was no knowing whether I would be able to return to my country after completing my term. My doubts were genuine for I had the case of Mohinder Singh before me. He was sentenced to fourteen years in 1953. His term was long since over but he was still languishing in jail as an internee.

Like me he had been taken prisoner at the age of twenty five and now he looked seventy. His beard and hair had turned gray and his youth had been eaten up by the jail. Thanks to our own government which allowed its subjects to rot in jail without caring to ascertain what kind of indignities they were undergoing in alien jails, for reasons exclusively patriotic.

New Jail Superintendent Welcomed

The Rajasthani dacoits, Thakur Jagmal Singh, Thakur Panna Singh, Thakur Mool Singh and two more prisoners who all belonged to the dacoit Madho Singh's gang were also lodged in the same prison with us. They used to carry on their depredations in the village on the border. After looting an Indian village they would slip into Pakistan and after raiding a Pak village they would take refuge in an Indian hide-out. They would kidnap the children of rich families and demand ransom from their parents. In India too there were heavy rewards on their heads. They had committed many murders.

Once when they raided a Pakistani village, the villagers fired in return, leading to indiscriminate exchange of fire. The Pakistani Border Rangers thought that Indian forces had mounted an attack on their territory and they swooped over the mauraders with helicopters. The dacoit Madho Singh was killed and five members of his gang were caught. They were awarded life imprisonment for dacoity in Pakistani territory.

In jail they had antagonised the Indian prisoners by their

habitual rude behaviour. They never missed an opportunity of bragging that they were dacoits. Though they behaved very nicely with Pakistani prisoners they regarded Indian prisoners as untouchables and would not even allow them touch their utensils. They proudly called themselves high class Hindus and considered us, the other Indian prisoners as Hindus of a low order. If an Indian prisoner happened to touch them they felt they had been defiled and this used to lead to violent outbursts.

By luring them with the offer of good food they had won some lackeys from among the Indian prisoners. They would put in hard labour on their behalf, act as their slaves and come to their succour in fights. The dacoits still had considerable money secreted somewhere and they possessed copies of the Gita and the Ramayana which they would not allow any Indian prisoner to touch.

When I came to Mianwali jail I was appalled at the behaviour of these dacoits and made no secret of it. I talked it over with my fellow Indian prisoners who were already prejudiced against se dacoits. The Indian prisoners were divided in two factions: the dacoits and their lackeys, numbering a dozen or so in all and about fifteen upright and well-meaning young prisoners who wanted to cut down these dacoits and their henchmen to size. The rest of the prisoners wanted to stay apart because of age, physical infirmity or ill-health. It appeared, we were heading for a show down

It was winter time. Chaudhri Naseer, the new Superintendent

had recently come on transfer from Lyallpur. Only a day previous to his arrival we had worked out a plan to deal with these people. Our group included Sadajeet Singh from Ferozpur, Lalchand from Ludhiana and ten more prisoners. We used to run our own kitchen where we had stocked sufficient logs of wood to stoke the *chulha*.

In the evening when Thakur Panna Singh was washing his utensils at the tap Sadajeet Singh went there to wash himself. Panna Singh immediately turned on him and started abusing him. To his utter surprise, Sadajeet Singh's clenched fist landed on his nose which sent him reeling. The other dacoits and their henchmen, hearing Panna Singh's cries, came running out of their cells to beat up Sadajeet Singh. All of us who were waiting just for that moment ran out armed with logs of firewood and felled the four dacoits who lay prostrate before us too dazed to know what had happened. They had no chance to offer resistance.

A nambardar who was on duty in the watch tower saw the melee from there and immediately sounded the alarm. The nambardars and the guards came out brandishing batons and lathis. But by then we had retreated into our barrack and locked its door from inside. Before the guards could come in by jumping over the wall we had found time enough to give a good hammering to the other companions of the dacoits who begged for mercy and promised that they would stop hobnobbing with these dacoits.

The nambardars who had come in by jumping over the walls were now upon us. We came in for some beating and half a dozen of us were taken away and locked up in the 'punishment room'. The dacoits were admitted into the jail hospital where they remained under treatment for over a month.

This was the Indian prisoners first salute to Superintendent Naseer who reciprocated by ordering that our feet should be chained and we should not be let out of our cells for four days. Our feet were accordingly shackled with thick chains, the heaviest that were available in the jail. The next 'gift' was that we were ordered to pound ten seers of munj each and make strings from it. Stones were dug into the floor for pounding the bamboo.

It was a sort of a convention in our barrack that only a newcomer to our barrack was asked to spin munj for fifteen days and after that he was not put to this kind of hard labour. To express our resentment we went on a hunger strike and refused to cook food in our kitchen. They could not beat us for going without food. It put Superintendent Naseer in a quandary. The Indian prisoners had become a pain in his neck. After three days he rescinded his order of spinning munj.

When the dacoits were discharged from the hospital they requested the Superintendent not to send them back to their old barrack. But the Superintendent did not agree. Within a month all their henchmen deserted them and came over to us.

The dacoits, totally demoralised, started living like lambs.

"We have only one request to make," they said. "We won't utter one word of abuse against you. But please don't touch our utensils." We conferred among ourselves. What objection could we have if these dacoits wanted to wallow in their own idiosyncracies? A truce was called and we decided to approach the Superintendent and request him to remove our shackles and take out the prisoners from the 'punishment' room.

At first Chaudhry Naseer would have none of it. Rather he expressed great indignation at our request. He said we were shameless brutes to fly at one another's throats. "Who would have been responsible if one of you had died?" he asked.

In the end he relented and ordered that our chains be removed. Our companions who were in the 'punishment' room were brought back to the barrack. We celebrated the event by cooking *halwā* in which the Thakurs also joined. There was eating and singing far into the night.

Our skirmish with the Thakurs had a salutary effect. The Pakistani prisoners began to respect us; they would not disdainfully brush us aside as they used to do before. Even the attitude of the jail staff towards us changed. Once again we started passing our days with dignity and in peace.

The Deputy Superintendent

We were passing our days in comparative peace when the Deputy Superintendent Fazaldad who had come on transfer from Montgomery descended upon us. Word had already reached us that he was very vindictive towards Indian prisoners; he would look out for opportunities to thrash them on the slightest pretext. A tailor by caste, burly, well trimmed beard, odd-featured, pot-belied, highly covetous, he would even fall for a bribe of two rupees. To our great misfortune, Chaudhri Naseer deputed him to take charge of our barrack.

He came to know I had been a school teacher. He seemed to have a special grudge against teachers. It was said that a school teacher whom he had engaged to coach his daughter at home had seduced her. He singled me out for his special attention. He had named me Pandit Murli Dhar. When he came to our barracks he would cry from a distance, "O, Pandit Murli Dhar, hold out your hand!" And he would start caning me on my extended palm, with great glee. It had almost become a pastime with him which he repeated every third or fourth day. Dacoit

Jagmal and others used to pass on a substantial portion of their rations to him. He had made dacoit Panna Singh my mate who used to provoke him against me and I often came in for beatings on that account.

Once a Muslim prisoner had fallen out with some other Muslim prisoners and feared that they may kill him. He was put in our barrack as a precautionary step against any such eventuality. His relative, Nabbu, a Pathan who was regarded as a terror at Mianwali and enjoyed the goodwill of a lot of people in jail was lodged in barrack No 3, which was adjacent to our barrack. He wanted the Muslim prisoner to be transferred to his barrack but the fellow did not agree and was consequently sent to our barrack. This prisoner was fairly educated and wanted to stay away from any kind of squabbles.

One day Fazaldad came to our barrack on his routine round and as usual started caning me to have his quota of fun. The Muslim prisoner who was new to our barrack and was not inured against such an outrageous behaviour objected. Intoxicated with power, Fazaldad failed to recognise the man and taking him for an Indian prisoner pounced upon him. The prisoner caught Fazaldad by the neck and giving him a violent push sent him crushing to the floor. A burly man, he fell like the effigy of Ravana. Pinning him down, the prisoner started pummelling him unmindful of the lathi blows from a nambardar. News spread to Nabbu in the adjacent barrack that a nambardar was beating his relative with the connivance of

Fazaldad. Nabbu rushed into the barrack with roughly fifty helpers, all armed with lathis and knives. All the four nambardars were severly beaten till they fainted. Some blows fell or Fazaldad too who was still lying prostrate on the ground. Nabbu wanted to knife him but his relative intervened.

The nambardar on the watch-tower saw the goings on and rang the alarm. All the prisoners climbed up on the roof to watch but we discreetly retired into our cells. On-such occasions, the guards generally rush in as a whirlwind taking everybody within sight in their sweep, not caring to ascertain who the real culprits are. Sometimes even prisoners sitting aloof and peacefully in their cells are not spared.

Dacoit Panna Singh took a wise step. Soon as we had returned to our cells he quickly locked the cells from outside.

Chaudhri Naseer thinking that the Indian prisoners had again fallen out among themselves and were creating this rumpus came abusing us from a distance. "Kill them! Break their bones! These wretched Indians can't digest their food in peace."

At the moment he reached our barrack, he found to his surprise that all of us were in our cells behind locked doors. Four nambardars were lying unconscious, drenched in blood. Fazaidad, who had gone into hiding came out on seeing the guards. He was in bad shape. He was still panting and his face and beard were covered with dust.

Chaudhri gradually came to know what had actually happened. He beat his head in despair. He knew that Nabbu was a power to reckon with and he did not want to take any false step at which the prisoners might go on further rampage. He tried to pacify Nabbu who kept insisting that it was a conspiracy against him in which Fazaldad had a hand and the whole matter must be thoroughly investigated by going down to its very roots. "At my call even the prisoners of the other barracks will climb up on the roof," he said. "You cannot gun down all of them?"

This was precisely what Chaudhri feared most and wanted to avoid. He promised that he would personally look into the whole matter and bring the culprits to book. Mollified, Nabbu came down from the roof with his followers.

After that Fazaldad never touched me. Gone was his swagger. In fact he was so much humiliated in our compound that he stopped visiting our barrack. If at all he would come, he quickly would go round and depart. For days we did not see Fazaldad's face. They say God's lathi makes no sound. Retribution had silently visited him and he had paid for his misdeeds. Thereafter whenever he came face to face with me he uttered kind words for me. I could see shadows of repentance on his face.

The festival of Baisakhi came. We were taken off our work that day and given extra rations. We had also collected some more from other sources. We put on clean clothes, sang bhajans, did *kirtan* and distributed halwa among the prisoners in the form of *prasad.* As a matter of courtesy we had also invited the jail staff though none came. If anybody came it was just out of curiosity to watch our religious customs. And then to our surprise we saw Fazaldad coming in simple clothes. He sa. down at the *kirtan* with us. It really took us all by surprise. At *ardas,* he stood up with us and it left us astounded when he raised his voice with us "Jo bole so nihal!" He held out his hand to receive the prasad and Sikh like, rubbed his greasy hands over his beard. Afterwards when Panna Singh offered him a plate of *halwa* he said, "Where's Pandit? I would rather have this plate from his hands." I felt gratified to oblige him. He took the plate and a spoon and went away.

Sheikh Mujib in Mianwali Jail

According to the news that had reached us Sheikh Mujib was supposed to be in the Lyallpur Jail. The winter had just started. A helicopter landed one night in our jail compound. We couldn't see who had got down from it, for our cells were locked at that time. In the morming we learnt that Sheikh Mujibur Rahman had been brought to Mianwali front the Lyalipur Jail. We also learnt that some soldiers of the East Bengal Regiment had dug a tunnel in the jail to whisk away the Sheikh from there but the attempt had proved abortive. He was lodged in the female ward of the Mianwali Jail, the women having been shifted to some other barrack. The female ward was right behind barrack No. 10.

We, the Indian prisoners were recently shifted to barrack No. 10 but we could not have a glimpse of him for he was being kept under a strong military guard. A Bengali cook had been assigned to him to cook his meals which consisted of fish and rice.

In the morning when the news of the Sheikh's arrival spread

in the jail the illiterate Pathan prisoners climbed up the roof of the jail barracks and shouted abuses at the Sheikh. They hurled rotten shoes and stones into the courtyard of the female ward some of which hit the military guards also.

The guards climbed up to the roof of the jail vestibule and fired six rounds in the air which terrified them enough to make them scamper down. But they continued to cat-call and abuse the Sheikh from their cells. Superintendent Chaudhri Naseer made a round of the barracks and told the prisoners that the Sheikh had been brought to the Mianwali Jail to be hanged. The Pakistani prisoners raised the cries of 'Ya Ali!' and jumped with joy.

We were eager to have a glimpse of Sheikh Mujib but there did not seem to be even a remote chance of our wish being realised. Here was a great hero, known as the Lion of Bengal who had awakened the hungry and oppressed people of East Bengal and had cheerfully sacrificed his family at the altar of freedom. According to the news circulating at that time it was said that even his son had been shot dead at the time of his arrest. Only his daughter Sheikh Hasina had escaped death.

We often saw his cook when we went to collect our rations. But we could not have a word with him because someone from the jail staff was always with him. The ration godown clerk would tauntingly ask the cook, "How's the traitor faring?" The cook would defiantly reply that the Sheikh was in fine health and sound in mind and would keep fighting for the rights of the Bengalis as long as there was breath in him.

One day the Deputy Superintendent Fazaldad came to our barrack with a nambardar and picked eight Indian prisoners at random from the first two cells, I being one of them. We were marched out and halted in front of the female ward where Sheikh Mujib was imprisoned. We were not told what was required of us nor did we care to find out. We were happy in the thought that we may yet be able to have a fleeting glimpse of the Sheikh. But to our chagrin even the wooden gate leading to his barred cell had been closed.

Fazaldad ordered us to dig an eight feet long four feet wide and four feet deep trench and specified the exact spot where the trench was to be dug. We immediately guessed that Sheikh Mujib was scheduled to be hanged that night and we were digging a grave to bury his dead body. Short of asking a question which we were reluctant to do, we had no way of confirming our suspicion.

The Pakistani prisoners, we realised, had deliberately been kept out of it lest the news should travel outside the jail through these prisoners.

The grave was ready by nine and we returned to our barrack, waiting with bated breath for the ominous news of Mujib's execution. Our ears were all along attuned to the 'house of death' but nothing happened throughout the night; everything was so quiet and still. It appeared that the decision to hang him had been deferred. But we were feeling apprehensive all the same for no one could understand the ways of the rulers. May be they had already strangled him to death in his room and then buried him by digging a hole through the floor. In the morning when our cells were unlocked we heard some people saying that Sheikh Mujib was still alive. Others said that some poison had been injected into his body putting him to eternal sleep after which he had been buried in the grave we had dug last evening. But these were all conjectures.

In the morning when we went to the ration godown to get our quota of ration we saw the Sheikh's cook waiting there to get milk, tea and sugar for the sheikh's morning tea. It meant that he was still alive.

It was rumoured that on the night of the Sheikh's execution Zulfikar Ali Bhutto had sought an audience with the President Yahya Khan and had advised him not to execute the Sheikh. He had impressed upon the President that if he was executed the Bengalis in East Pakistan would not sit idle. The Pakistani forces stationed in East Pakistan right from the highest officer down to the jawan would become the target of their wrath. They would not even spare their children Acting on Bhutto's advice, Yahya Khan had stopped Mujib's execution.

The next day we were again called out and were asked to fill up the trench we had dug the previous day. We were happy that even indirectly we were not made a party to this crime. But our happiness was short-lived.

Fifteen days later we were again called out and asked to dig a similar trench. But this time again Sheikh Mujib was not hanged. This process was repeated three times and every time his hanging was deferred. In this manner Sheikh Mujib stayed for four months in the Mianwali Jail. His Bengali cook was very devoted to him. When he came to the ration godown we could see that he wished to speak to us but it was difficult for him to open his lips under such heavy guard.

As luck would have it, Sheikh Mujibur-Rahman was four times saved from mounting the gallows. Previous to this he had been put behind the bars in connection with the Agartala Conspiracy Case. Even at that time Field Marshal Mohammed Ayub Khan wanted to execute him but had let him off on the advice of Bhutto. Later, when Bangladesh was born he became its first President. But nobody could believe that the same people for whom he had made such huge sacrifices and suffered imprisonment and humiliation would so outrageously do him to death.

A few months before the murder of Mujib when he was the President of Bangladesh our Indian agency RAW (Research & Analysis Wing) had got an inkling of unrest in the Bangladesh army. At that time when the conspiracy for the assassination of President Mujib was being hatched an officer of the Bangladesh army who had been bought over by our government was also present. He had secretly scribed down some notes on a small slip of paper and casually dropped it into the wastepaper basket from where it was retrieved by one of our agents and dispatched to New Delhi. It contained the warning that the army was planning to kill Mujib.

R.N. Kao, the chief of RAW came to Bangladesh in the guise of a betel leaf seller. He managed a secret meeting with Mujib where he warned him of the impending danger to his life. Mujib bad taken it very lightly and said, "How can that be? They are like my own children. They will never kill me." By warning Sheikh Mujib the Indian Government had done its duty and the rest was up to Mujib.

Mujib was assassinated along with his entire family at the hand of Zia-ur-Rahman, the chief of the Bangladesh army. Even now the days that Sheikh Mujib spent in the Mianwali Jail keep haunting me. Time and again they would prepare the noose for his neck and dig a grave to receive his lifeless body. But he did not die at the hands of his enemies. He died at the hands of his own people whom he called his children. It is truly said that the wolves of fate keep a man on the run all his life. They tire him and when he is down and out they tear him apart and devour him.

The Nights of the 1971 War

The conditions in Bangladesh had deteriorated beyond redemption but in Pakistan preparations for war were in full swing. The airfield at Mianwali was right behind the jail where every day Mirage aircrafts took off. And then there were Chinese planes taking off from Sakesar which was quite close to Mianwali. It appeared that the armies would dash on the Western front.

The population of Mianwali mostly comprises of rustic Pathans. They either join the army or take to crime. We learnt from the visitors who came to meet the prisoners that their relatives in the army had been sent to the front. The winter had set in. The months of September, October and November passed uneventfully. Since the creation of Pakistan the tension between the two countries along their borders was always there and had therefore no special significance. Even if there was a routine movement of forces along the respective borders people thought that it was precursor to war.

From the Ist of December black-out exercises were

introduced on regular intervals to the civil population. Even on the evening of 3rd December when we were confined to our cells we were not prepared to believe that war would break out on the Western Sector. But at about three in the morning our sleep was disturbed by the roars of army planes. I could recognise the sound of Canberras – our Indian bombers. I told my Indian companions excitedly, "There come our bombers!"

My companion, Sohanlal, was not convinced. "Don't talk rubbish," he said. "They are Pakistani planes engaged in air exercises." He had not even finished speaking when we heard the Pakistani anti-aircraft guns, which were fixed all round the airfield, cracking away.

There were twelve guns firing simultaneously. The Canberras had started bombing the airfield while the Gnats which had accompanied the bombers had opened machine gun fire to silence the anti-aircraft guns. The bombing by the Canberras shook the mud walls of the jail. Birds which had built nests under our roof fell down along with the nests. One of our companions, Raghbir Singh shouted, "India Zindabad!" But I immediately placed my hand over his mouth. "Son, keep quiet," I warned him. "Otherwise these uncouth Pathans will make *murdabad* of all of us before the sun rises.

The anti-aircraft guns soon fell silent. In the morning we were subjected to a vigorous search. It was a windfall for Fazaldad. He rummaged through our canisters and carried away everything that he could lay his hands upon – gur, sugar, tea

248

leaves, cigarettes. "You scoundrels have been guiding those planes with your cigarette lights," he complained. It made us laugh. How could our lights penetrate the barrack roof? It was an excuse to take away our things. Which fool would invite death by exposing his location to a bombing plane which in our case could have made no distinction between friend and fce?

Now the Indian planes began making air sorties every two hours. They completely damaged the runway at Mianwali and Sakesar. They would hover over these airfields like homing pigeons while the Radio Pakistan blared forth news of its victories. When I heard Radio Pakistan announcing that the Pakistani forces had penetrated twenty-five miles into the Indian territory near the Ferozpur border I felt terribly scared. My home was only five miles from the border.

Sometimes we managed to get the real picture through the visitors of our Pakistani prisoner friends. We learnt that Indian forces had penetrated sixty miles into the Pakistani territory in the Sialkot sector and our navy had wrought havoc at the Karachi harbour. We also learnt that the Pakistani submarine 'Ghazi' had met its watery grave at the hands of the Indian Navy.

The Pakistanis themselves admitted that India was too mighty a power for Pakistan to successfully fight against it. Every night when we were locked into our cells we found ourselves between two cross-fires. We feared lest we should become the targets of the Indian bombers who were often seen hovering over the jail barracks. And there were heavy locks outside the barrack doors to prevent us from running out for safety in case of bombing.

The jail walls shook under the impact of each bombing. Mianwali airfield being just behind the jail it could any time become the target of air attack. Amusingly enough, and to our great relief we were no longer put to hard labour. We spent the whole day gossiping. Our cells were not locked during the day and we would sit outside joyously watching the Indian aircrafts coming in. At that time the Pakistani prisoners would disappear into their cells for shelter.

Death loomed as large over them as it did over us. We laughed over it while they put on rueful expressions and scurried for shelter on every occasion. The planes would just hurl down bombs and fly away while we would gaze at them wistfully awaiting their return to bombard the enemy again.

One day Fazaldad and Malik Ata Mohammed came for a round at about eleven in the morning. They had not finished when the planes arrived. Malik Ata Mohammed was quite young. He jumped out of our barrack in one bound and hid somewhere in the firing range of the jail circuit. But the burly Fazaldad ran hetter-sketter, looking for a refuge. Rising and falling he entered our cell. He had made quite a spectacle of himself. Then the walls of our cell started shaking and he feared that the roof may crash upon him. He again ran out and took refuge is one of the *pucca* latrines in the compound.

Our sides split with laughter but we tried to control ourselves for we knew of Fazaldad's vile, vengeful nature. Ten minutes after the departure of the planes he emerged from the latrine, hitching up his pants. He cut such a ludicurous figure.

In those days we were awfully short of cigarettes and tea. Sometimes a friend would pick up half-smoked cigarette stubs from another barrack. We would wrap the stub in a leaf and sitting in a line we would take a puff at it one after the other. No one was permitted to take more than one puff. If anyone tried to violate the rule all of us would shower abuses at him. It presented even a grimmer proposition. We would even use tree bark for tea leaves, boil it in water and drink the concoction, after adding sugar to it. Not that we did not enjoy it for it had a peculiar taste of its own. Even today when I drink tea I remember that concoction.

Night was still more difficult for we were not allowed to keep matches with us. But we had improvised automatic lighters of our own. We would burn raw yarn and keep it in a used boot polish tin. We had picked up pieces of flint from outside and had fixed them in a piece of wood. When we struck it against a stone it let off sparks which fell on the raw yarn and ignited it. We would light our stubs and close the box, thereby extinguishing the yarn.

Smoking a cigarette was as much a problem as lighting it. Every one of us would go to a corner across which we had a blanket to improvise a urinal, take a drag at the stub and return to his place. The stubs were too small to be smoked properly. We devised a method out of this difficulty by rolling sheets of paper into cheroots, stuffing them with tobacco taken from small stubs and smoking these so called cheroots. In our compound one cell had been converted into a cigarette factory. While sweeping the compound we would collect all the stubs and send them to the 'factory' as the raw material for cigarettes. Each cell was entitled to two cheroots per night. These nights of 1971 still haunt me whenever I take out a cigarette to smoke.

Back to Multan

The war was in its tenth day when on the 13th December orders were received to transfer all Indian prisoners to the Multan Jail. The guards were soon on their job and handcuffed the right and the left hands of two prisoners together so that we moved in pairs. It was quite a job to lift our canisters with shackled hands. But as we came out of the jail vestibule, to our great delight, we saw two special buses waiting outside the jail to carry us away. A special guard had been deputed to escort us.

Some of our companions had grown long hair and had elaborately tied their turbans in Sikh style. We had warned them just to coil the turbans over their heads for one could never predict the local people's mood and something untoward could happen on the way. But they did not pay any heed to our warning. We set off on our journey at ten.

Our buses had hardly gone some distance when the Indian planes appeared in the sky and our buses had to take cover under the trees. We had felt the effects of the Indian air attack while inside the jail but now we were witnessing it from outside the four walls of the jail. The faces of our drivers turned pale and they frantically started intoning the stock prayer to ward off the danger from over their heads. The guards to whose belts our handcuffs were chained were equally jittery.

"Why are you feeling so scared?" we asked them. "Our lives can also be blasted out along with yours."

"Being prisoners you are already as good as dead," they retorted. "You will welcome death. But we have our families to live for."

Though highly amused, we thought there was no point in pulling their legs and let the matter drop at that.

We heard loud blasts at the Mianwali railway station followed by huge flares and then saw dense smoke billowing up. It appeared a train had been bombed and it had caught fire. The planes had safely got away after doing their job. Strangely enough, we did not see a single Pakistani aircraft taking off from the Mianwali and Sakesar airfields during those early days of the war. The only explanation we could think of was that either the Pakistani planes had been knocked out on the ground or the runways had been damaged beyond repair. Even if they undertook repairs they would have to reckon with further air attacks which always had a strong deterrent factor. We wanted to have a good look at what was going on around us but the guards spoiled our fun by ordering the buses to resume their journey.

It was about an eight to ten hours journey and the buses

were not to stop anywhere on the way. Somewhere near Azamgarh, a place on this side of Multan, we requested the Guard Commander to stop the buses for a while so that we could ease ourselves but he refused to consider our request. But at Azamgarh the guards themselves stopped the buses to go to the urinals. The tea stall owner there was a kindly sort of man and he said he would serve us tea before we resumed our journey. While we were, waiting for the tea to be ready people started gathering round our buses. Going by the Sikh turbans they thought that we were Indian soldiers freshly taken prisoners and started shooting 'Ya Ali!' in their excitement and some of them even took to pelting stones at us. Leaving their tea unfinished, the guards rushed in to our protection.

"You sons of dogs!" they cried while chasing away the crowd with butts of their guns, "You put your tails between your legs and run away from the battle-field and yet think yourselves to be brave enough to be able to throw stones at unarmed people,"

The buses started immediately and pushing the crowd behind, the guards jumped into the running vehicles.

We were outside the gate of the Multan Jail at five. It is considered to be the most notorious jail of Pakistan. Jahangir Hathiana, its Superintendent was a wild, brute of a man who was said to have a stone in place of a heart. It is said that when a buffalo pulling a cart laden with rations bellowed in the jail be ordered it to be given thirty lashes. It was also said that two prisoners who had not mended their ways in spite of persistent flogging were ordered to be pushed into the raging oven fire and were subsequently accounted for as escapees from jail. Even after intensive enquiry no guilt could be established against the Superintendent and he got away with impunity. A l prisoners used to pray that they be saved from the wrath of Hathiana. And now as our luck would have it, we were put face to face with this brute.

We were thoroughly searched in the jail vestibule. They could not find anything incriminating in our possession. The nambardars pushed us into barrack No. 3 located in the wing meant for those condemned to death. The entire jail was a two-storied affair made of bricks, and the war being on, the prisoners were kept locked in their cells. It was the responsibility of us, Indians, to sweep and wipe the floors, two prisoners each being assigned to sweep and wipe the barracks of huge dimensions. In spite of our repeated requests we were not allowed to start a kitchen of our own. The Pakistani prisoners cooked the *daal* for us and out of sheer cussedness they would sometimes put pieces of meat and bones in *daal*. We had complained about it on several occasions but Hatthiana had brushed aside these as frivolous.

We were put in the cells on the upper floor while the prisoners condemned to death were lodged on the ground floor. We were not permitted to talk to them and if the nambardar caught us doing so we were in for trouble. We had one Pandit Sitaram of Amritsar with us. His real name was Jai Ram or

Lakshman Das but he was known to us by his assumed name.

We had been in the Multan Jail only for five days when we learnt that the Pakistani army in Bangladesh had laid down its arms. General Yahya Khan had been put under house arrest by General Gul Hasan. Tikka Khan and Zulfikar Ali Bhutto had taken the reins of the country in their hands. The backbone of the Pakistanis had broken but that had increased their hatred against us. The nambardars would flare up against us at the smallest pretext. Out of sheer spite Hathiana had put us on the job of pounding munj and making string out of it. On the fourth day of our assignment he came to our barracks on inspection. He was still making his round when Pandit Sitaram ran after him brandishing the wooden rod used for pounding munj. Although his feet were shackled and the nambardar who had been beating him with his baton had felled him to the ground, Pandit Sitaram still kept fulminating against Hathiana. "You rascal, you make us eat bones in our *daal* and then you have the cheek to ask us to pound munj!"

The Pandit was given a sound beating for three consecutive days. When he fainted he would be thrown in a water cistern. The nambardars asked him to beg Hathiana's pardon but he refused. Luckily for him, just then orders came for transfer of some of the prisoners to the Mianwali Jail and the Pandit happened to be one of them. A good many of my companions had gone back to Mianwali, but many of us, myself included, were left behind to put up with Hathiana's harassment.

A Tunnel in Multan Jail

Our companions having gone to Mianwali, only eight of us were left behind. In the barrack right below our own there were one hundred and twenty-seven Pakistani prisoners awaiting execution. When the 1971 war started the execution of these prisoners was stayed. But with the termination of the war orders for their execution again started pouring in.

These prisoners were already fed up with Hathiana's wantonness. At that time the dacoit Mohammed Khan was also in the same jail and had been awarded death sentence in seven cases. There was no possibility of his being saved from death. So he worked out a plan to make an escape from jail. During the course of the war the vigilance squad of the jail had become lax in its duties. First, Mohammed Khan smuggled in pistol parts hidden under frozen ghee, through his friend He assembled the parts into pistols with fairly satisfactory results. Soon a stage was reached when every fifth prisoner surreptitiously came to possess a free pistol. As for knives, each one of them had one.

One day the prisoners of all the barracks went after the jail staff with knives and started firing in the air. The Jail Superintendent Hathiana was taken by surprise. He was caught between two opposing forces. Now the prisoners held full sway within the jail and the police outside it. The prisoners had got rid of their shackles in the jail workshop and forged spears, arrows and bows from them and additionally from the iron railings uprooted from the jail. They had virtually converted the jail into a fortress in which they were feeling very safe and secure.

To harass the prisoners the authorities had withdrawn the scavengers from the jail. At this the prisoners started we going to the jail gate in batches of ten to ease themselves. Soon the place started stinking, making it impossible for the jail staff to work in the jail office. The jail authorities debarred the visitors from meeting the prisoners. In the end, the jail authorities were themselves forced to make arrangements to clean up the place and resume scavenging services. The things brought by the visitors were also duly delivered to the prisoners.

The Pakistani prisoners who had been condemned to death went into a huddle with the Indian prisoners and it was decided to dig a tunnel in the jail. Of course, it was to be a hushed-up affair so that nobody should get wind of it except those who were to be directly involved in it.

The barrack No. 3 had a stage in front of it where plays

were performed for the entertainment of prisoners. There was a three hundred feet long and two hundred feet wide slightly raised platform in front of the stage from where the spectators watched the play. There was also a green room adjacent to the stage for necessary make-up etc. It was decided to stall the tunnel from under that green room and the job of digging the tunnel was entrusted to Indian prisoners, Rajinder who was a resident of Jammu, Ashok of Ferozpur, Charan Singh Dhullar of Amritsar, Tilakraj Joshi and others, numbering twelve in all. It was decided that on completion of the tunnel the Indian prisoners would take the lead. They would make a bid to get across the border along with the Pakistani prisoners.

The work on the tunnel started. Two men dug the earth and two men carried away the earth. In this manner three parties worked on a four hour shift each. The earth dug out of the tunnel was evenly spread on the platform in front of the stage. We, the Indian prisoners received the special attention of our counterparts and were duly feted by them. They provided us with chicken, meat, zarda, pullav, halwa and sweets through their visitors. We had now been on the job for a fortnight. We did not confront any serious problem for there had been no administrative control over the jail for almost a month and a quarter.

Perhaps this was the first instance in the history of jails that one of its units should have left its prisoners to their own devices for such a long stretch of time, and the irony of it was that this had happened in the regime of a jail officer who was regarded as the most autocratic of jail officials in Pakistan.

The work of digging the tunnel was done under the overall supervision of dacoit Mohammed Khan. We had dug the tunnel to a length of 150 feet or so and had made an opening in one of the fields beyond the jail walls. We covered the mouth of the tunnel with a large piece of stone and came away.

We celebrated the occasion with great eclat, sang songs and did a bhangra dance. We had to finish all the rations left in our canisters. Two in the night, the time at which the moon disappeared, was decided upon as the hour of escape. Mohammed Khan went to the vestibule to meet a visitor and returned after an hour.

All of us retired at eight to snatch as much sleep as we could. We had to walk a long way through the night to gain the border. But we were too excited to sleep. We were happy in the thought that we would soon be gaining freedom. At the same time we were full of trepidation lest our efforts should come to naught.

To our utter surprise we saw that at quarter to two the high jail walls which in jail parlance were called 'kotmoka' were flooded with high power bulbs. The hearts of the prisoners started pounding hard. What were they up against? Had the jail authorities got wind of our plan to stage an escape? Who could the traitor be? The prisoners came out of their barracks, grimly resolved to fight it out to the bitter end with the police. It could never occur to anyone of us that the dacoit Mohammed Khan who had been awarded death sentence in seven cases could have himself betrayed us.

In that strong electric light we saw machine guns positioned on the jail walls. Then came a warning over the mike, asking every prisoner to surrender his arms and get back into his cell. Any one found violating this order, the warning said, would be shot dead.

At three the jail gate flung open and two battalions of the Pakistani army – perhaps they were the 9th Baluch and the 13th Punjab – marched firing shots in the air. The prisoners were in jitters. Knives and pistols could be no match to .303 and LMG rifles. Even so, some of the prisoners had the gumption to fire their pistols from the roof tops of their barracks.

By now the military had entered the barracks and was mowing down indiscriminately any one who came within its sight. Prisoners were dragged out of their cells and their limbs broken. Jahangir had recently been transferred and Haji Iftikhar Khan was directing the operations. About 157 prisoners were killed and 262 prisoners were crippled.

A list of the rebels had been furnished to the jail authorities through Mohammed Khan An order blared forth through the mike: "Prisoner Mohammed Aziz, come out of the barrack within three minutes holding your hands up. Otherwise you will be shot dead in the barrack!" As the prisoner came out the guards pounced upon him and started beating him. They kept at it till he fell down unconscious. They had particularly aimed their lathis at his arms and legs with a view to permanently cripple him. Then he was dragged away and thrown into the jail hospital. As an afterthought, it was decided to do away with these people. They were again dragged out of the jail and shot dead.

In each barrack all the prisoners came in for their attention. After finishing with the ground floor they came to the first floor. The police guards were going to pull out the Indian prisoners when Haji Iftikhar intervened. "They are a decent lot," he said. "I know them since my Lahore days. Don't beat them."

"But they are the main culprits responsible for digging the tunnel," the Deputy Superintendent objected.

"It's all tommy rot," Haji Iftikhar countered. "I don't believe a word of it."

The police guard came down from the Indian barrack without doing any harm to the Indian prisoners. None of them was even slapped.

Later on the Indian prisoners were put on the job of cleaning up the jail. There was blood all over the place, The dead bodies had been removed but one could still hear groans and cries emanating from all the barracks. Haji Iftikhar personally examined the tunnel and the press photographers took its photographs. For two days the Multan Jail Tunnel episode remained in the limelight in the radio broadcasts all over the world.

Three days later the Pakistani Ministers Janab Qauser Niazi and Mohammed Ali Kasuri came on an official visit and asked the prisoners the reasons why they had rebelled. The prisoners in the 'penal' barrack narrated to them harrowing tales of torture which would make one's flesh creep. They were systematically beaten three times a day with old shoes made from leather straps. They also showed the ministers a nine-inch long piece of wood carved in the shape of a penis which was oiled and thrust into their anus every morning.

Perhaps no other jail in the world subjected its prisoners to such hideous indignity. But in the Multan Jail, Jahangir Hathiana did it at the slightest provocation without turning a hair. The two ministers were also shown some very young boys who had been subjected to sexual assaults by jail sweepers under orders of Hathiana. The entire Pakistani press mounted a virulent attack against Hathiana. Qauser Niazi and Mohammed Ali Kasuri were apologetic and agreed that it was but natural for the prisoners to rebel under such barbarous treatment. They assured the prisoners that such a thing would not happen again.

The prisoners were given new uniforms and new blankets. The sick and the wounded were given proper medical treatment and no prisoner was put to hard labour for a month. Following this episode orders were passed for transfer of the Indian prisoners to the Mianwali Jail. We were happy to meet our old friends again and we regaled them with stories from our Multan experiences.

Return to Mianwali

We were happy at having been pulled out of a dirty hole like Multan and be back to the Mianwali Jail. Taking a cue from other jails the prisoners in the Mianwali Jail had also become bold and spirited. Bird fights and sodomy had become common pastimes. They knifed each other at the slightest provocation, gambled and squabbled with the wardens for fun. Here a dacoit, Ghulan Rasool, ruled the roost. He had twelve 'boys' with whom he slept turn by turn.

When a young boy came to jail the rakes and the roughs among the prisoners would vie with each other as to by whose side the boy's charpoy would be spread. The hardened ones would even brandish knives to intimidate the others. Most of these boys were loafers, pickpockets, petty thieves and touts. Being bad characters themselves they did not mind being roughed up in jail. On the contrary, they rather relished jail life for the peaceful time that it promised them. They would also get good things to eat – chicken, mutton, nice vegetable curries besides perfumed soaps and oils for bath.

These self-styled jail lords kept these boys decked out like sweethearts – they were called the 'fairies' of the jail. Wherever they passed, perfume wafting from their clothes hung in the air. I have not seen even college girls behaving so coyly. Wearing flamboyant coloured kurtas and small salwars, well groomed curly hair falling over their necks, their eyes thinly streaked with kajal and a partridge perched on their hand, they would walk swaying their hips, like the denizen of a Mughal King's harem. So much so that they wore knitted pajama cords, pearls hanging from their taselled ends.

In our barrack many of our Indian brethren such as Pandit Ashwani Kumar, Lalchand, Mahboob Massih, Sadajit Singh, Mohammeddin, knitted tasselled pajama cords and did embroidery work on them and embellished them with pearls. These pajama cords were in great demand and their prices ranged between six to sixteen rupees each. Our barrack had become a sort of pajama cord manufacturing 'factory'. Our products were even fancied by the jail officers' wives and daughters and we had to pander to their whims.

Our barrack was also the centre for the sale of opium and hemp. Babu Madan Gopal and myself supervised the sale of these narcotics. We had four underlings working for us and we bore the expenses of their cigarettes, tea, oil and soap, etc. It was their job to effect clandestine sale of these narcotics on our behalf by going round the jail barracks and ferreting out the potential customers. They were quite adept in sizing up such people. Even if caught and beaten they would not divulge our names.

Apart from that, Babu Madan Gopal and myself studied palms and made predictions mainly based on astrology. We would let off one and hang the other. In that highly populated jail our predictions were bound to come true in one case or the other which helped to build up our reputation. We thus managed to make many devotees through sheer nuke. They would express their gratitude by offering us cigarettes, ghee, sugar, fruits, tea, sweets and even cash which we shared with our friends and cronies.

Pandit Om Prakash and Vasdev were very good at hair cutting. Even prisoners from other barracks came to them and paid for hair cuts. Balbir from Ferozpur was running a shoe mending unit and did brisk business. Hanuman Prashad from Rajasthan was an excellent tailor. He could even stitch a woollen suit without recourse to the sewing machine. Once the Jail Superintendent had all his daughter's clothes for her wedditig stitched by him.

Mahboob Massih, apart from making pajama cords was good at dispensing medicines. He would get a variety of pills from the jail hospital and keep them handy with him. For instance, he had sulphaguanidine for dysentery, enterovioform for stomach troubles and dysentery, APC powder for fever, quinine for malaria, and butabarbitone for insomnia. In short, Massih had medicine for almost every ailment which we used to get at all odd hours. For this reason, the inmates of the jail tried to remain very friendly with him. Some of the prisoners of our barrack had managed to put by so much money that they had even taken to gambling. In jail, gambling was done mostly with the help of Ludo dice which had a maximum of six dots on one of its sides.

Once Tilakraj Joshi of Amritsar won a hundred rupees at one sitting but he refused to call it a day. In the end he returned to his barrack minus three hundred rupees. Similar was the case with Pandit Avinash Kumar of Ludhiana. Whatever he earned by making pajama cords he would lose it at the gambling counter. Eventually he gave up playing. Baba Takhtmal had very nimble fingers; he stole without one being the wiser for it. But he was fond of opium and was often beaten on that account but he refused to give up the habit. Buta Massih, another inmate of our barrack was an incorrigible miser and cantankerous type. He would keep his own things under lock and key and then unabashedly beg for cigarettes and other things from others, saying that his own stock was finished.

Having a propensity to steal, Baba Takhtmal would keep an eye on others' things. One evening when Buta Massih had gone out to beg for cigarettes from other prisoners, as if by a sleight of hand, Baba Takhtmal stole his entire stock of cigarettes. He went round hawking the cigarettes from barrack to barrack and in no time managed to sell sixty packets in twelve barracks at whatever they fetched and quietly pocketed the money and later utilised it for buying opium from me. When Buta Massih returned to his barrack and found his box of cigarettes lying empty on the floor he started wailing at his loss.

"But you said that you had no cigarettes," the other prisoners "Where did your stolen cigarettes come from?"

Baba Takhtmal removed his shoe and started beating Buta Massih with it. "Sala, first you beg from us and then call us thieves!" he cried. To add to the fun, some of the stolen cigarettes fell from Baba Takhtmal's pocket while he was be labouring Buta Massih and a lunatic in our barrack swooped upon them, making a mess of all things.

To our amusement, angered at their accidental losses both of them started fighting and we disengaged these old foggies with great difficulty and locked them up in separate cells.

For once we were having a pleasant time in jail when the Pakistani prisoners struck a discordant note. They refused to put in hard labour and advised us to do likewise. At our refusal they turned hostile to us, called us traitors and drove us away whenever we wanted to accost them.

They stopped getting their jobs done by us as a result of which our remunerative activities came to a standstill and our stocks gradually depleted. They would not even permit us to pick up cigarette stubs and would throw them into the gutters so that they became totally useless to us. To make things worse, there was no discipline in the jail and we felt miserable, wondering how we would pass our days in such chaos.

In Mianwali

The vagaries of the Pakistani prisoners had crossed all limits. No hard labour, gambling throughout the day, tiffs with the wardens, brandishing knives at each other. Some of them even had pistols smuggled in by bribing outsiders. Unbelievably one or two even possessed sten guns. The dacoit Ghulam Hasan every day filched fives seers ghee, ten seer gur, one kilo tea and a substantial quantity of daal from the jail godown at the point of his pistol. He had set up a gambling den within the jail premises and sent five hundred rupees to his home every month.

It was around that time that the People's Party came into power and Mohammed Hakim Amin Khan took charge of jail administration. A resident of Campbellpur, he was originally a police havaldar and being an office bearer of the People's Party had reached this high office. The Campbellpur area was notorious for crime and some of the minister's relatives were also locked up in jails. Having been a police havaldar, he knew how to deal with goondas.

One morning at five, the jail barracks resounded with sudden thuds of heavy boots of guards. Then about fifteen hundred armed soldiers entered the jail. Half of them climbed up the roofs and the other half proceeded for a man to man search of the prisoners. They would kick the cell door open, strip the prisoners of all his clothes except the underwear, toll-up all his belongings in his blanket and send it to the ration godown. Then the prisoners were subjected to severe lathi blows to find out where they had hidden their knives and firearms.

Jail Superintendent, Chaudhri Naseer, a barber by caste, had shown great patience towards these recalcitrant prisoners and had given them sufficient time to mend their ways. But these stupid fellows had paid no heed to him. They thought the jail was their playground. Now they were whining before the soldiers and in order to avoid further kicks, they were taking out the firearms from their hidden places. They were even peeking against their own fellow prisoners.

Soldiers were particularly severe with those who plundered the jail rations. They beat them with lathis, stripped them of their clothes and then pushed them into their cells naked. Even their mugs and tumblers were taken away from them so that they could not even have a drink of water.

In the course of their search they came to barrack No. 10, where we, the Indian prisoners were lodged. We remonstrated with the soldiers that we were alien prisoners and we had no firearms with us for we believed in abiding by the jail regulation.

The Jail Superintendent, Chaudhri Naseer came to our rescue in the nick of time. He firmly told the soldiers that he was running the jail administration through our help and cooperation. "These people are looking after the jail sanitation," he told them. "But for them, worms would have been crawling here long ago." Some Indian prisoners were beaten by mistake. They were promptly sent to the jail hospital for treatment. They were kept them for a week and given half seer milk every day.

The articles wrenched off from the Pakistani prisoners consisting of cigarettes, gur, ghee, sugar, tea leaves, chillies, salt, utensils, sweaters, mufflers, coats, pants and salwar-kamiz were heaped outside the ration godown. They could have filled ten trucks. We were asked to sort out these articles and prepare their inventories. It proved a windfall to the jail wardens. The best of the quilts, blankets, and bedsheets and tins of pure ghee were sent to the chief warden's and the deputy superintendent's houses. The other things were thrown over the jail walls to be collected by the relatives of the wardens who were waiting for them to carry away to their homes. As for us, every evening we were given one seer each of gur, a substantial quantity of tea leaves and cigarettes besides betel leaves laced with tobacco as a reward for our gesture of good behaviour and services rendered.

It being winter, every Indian prisoner was given two heavy sweaters, one muffler and one kurta-pajama. We seemed to have turned the tables on the Pakistani prisoners. While our canisters were once again stocked full with much wanted commodities, the Pakistani prisoners went about looking for measly cigarette stubs. We were entrusted with the sanitation of the fort and eight Pakistani prisoners holding brooms and scrubbers were placed under the command of each Indian prisoner. They would fill the drum with dirty water scooped out the gutter and sprinkle it over the floors and sweep them clean. All that we did was to blithely puff at our cigarettes and keep an eye on them while they worked. We remembered the time, only a month ago, when the Pakistani prisoners would not even allow us to pick up cigarette stubs from the ground to smoke. We really pitied them when they begged us for half-smoked cigarettes. Ghulam Hasan's lot, who boasted of having twelve gigolos was the worst. It was the same with 90 per cent of the other Pakistani prisoners. First Ghulam Hasan was given a good beating by the guards, then his head was shaved and face blackened. He was mounted on a donkey with a pot of excreta placed on his head and taken round the barracks as an exhibit. The round over, the guards stripped him of all his clothes, making him stark naked and made all his gigolos mount on him one by one. Soon after he was transferred to the Khiarpur Jail. It is better left to one's imagination as to how the fifty-five year old, long moustached Ghulam Hasan, at whose very name the jail population trembled with fear, must have felt at being rubbed the wrong way so challengingly.

No prisoner was allowed to meet another for twenty days. After that period, when visits were resumed half the quantity of the things that the visitors brought with them was usurped by the jail staff right in the vestibule. No prisoner was allowed to have more than three packets of cigarettes per week. To carry matches on one's person was strictly forbidden. One had to beg the nambardar or a warden for matches to light a cigarette. As against this we, the Indians, had cigarette lighters and imported ones at that which they pilfered from the confiscated goods. Nobody ever bothered us for the Superintendent Naseer Ahmed and the Chief Warden, Sher Khan, were very kind to us.

Apart from cigarettes, as I have already said, the visitors could only bring in sweets and fruits of which half the quantity was taken away by the jail staff. Of what was left they parted with some of it in our favour, by way of a bribe so that we should not be severe with them while exacting work from them. It was indeed an anamolous situation. While they scooped out dirty water from the drains we happily ate their grapes, pomegrantes, oranges, apples and sweets.

Every prisoner was given ten seers munj to pound and make strings from it. It was like asking a prostitute to grind corn. The prisoners whimpered as they worked. Having led an easy life in jail they had become work-shy and now could not cope with this kind of strenuous work. As such most of the prisoners came in for a beating in the evening. They would cry before

Chaudhri Naseer and beg for his mercy, assuring him that they would not break the jail rules in future ever again and behave like harmless lambs. It was the same jail superintendent whom the prisoners used to call 'the barber' in derision. But Chaudhri would refuse to relent. As compared to the Indians who were highly disciplined, these Pakistani prisoners were a spoiled lot and Chaudhri wanted to teach them permanent lessons.

The Chief Warden Shera

Of those who were considerate to the Indian prisoners and stood by them in times of difficulty one cannot forget the name of the Chief Warden, Mohammed Sher Khan, or Shera for short. He treated the Indian prisoners like his own sons. He had ordered that the prisoners' leg chains be removed and he allowed them to move about in all the barracks. The Indian prisoners used to call him Chacha Shera and he would reciprocate by calling them 'my lions' which meant my brood of lions. If the Pakistani prisoners did not find themselves upto a job he would entrust the job to the Indian prisoners, confident that they would deliver the goods.

It rained heavily one night and half the roof of barrack No. 4 caved in. The prisoners in that barrack were to be shifted urgently to another barrack the same night. The number of prisoners in the jail was far beyond its capacity. If government tenders had been called, as per the set procedure, it would have taken many months to replace the roof. To save time, Shera put the Indian prisoners on the job of repairing the roof.

Amrik Singh, alias Kishori Lal of Jalandhar, was a good mason and quick at work. He had also trained Ashok Kumar and Rajinder Kumar of Jammu in this job. In a jiffy, seventy Indians were placed on the job under Amrik Singh's supervision. Even the insane among us were asked to lend a helping hand. Within three days fifteen cells of the barrack had been repaired and made ready for the prisoners to move in.

As if obliged, the Jail Superintendent rewarded us with a set of new clothes each, new bedsheets and double rations. We were also served specal tea while at work.

Shera would generally entrust us with some kind of work that would recoil to our benefit. For instance, if a truck-load of gur arrived he would put us on the job of unloading the truck. On our finishing the job he would put two seers of gur each in our laps. One day he found that four walls of the jail which were called 'kot mauka' had started crumbling in places. All the walls required to be plastered with mud. The job was again entrusted to us. Fazaldad was the over-all incharge of 'kot mauka' and on the first day, by way of hard labour, he ordered twelve of us who had been put on this job, to plaster a 60 feet length of the wall upto a height of 18 feet.

We had to work under the blazing sun. Shera told Fazaldad that it would not be possible for us to complete this lengthy assignment by evening. "You're always partial to these Indians," Fazaldad taunted Shera.

"Don't worry, Chacha," we told Shera to save the situation. "We shall see to it that the job is finished by evening."

Two people started kneading the mud while six of us were assigned to carry the mud upstairs. Similarly, two people rolled the drums to the top via the flight of stairs while two people filled them with water before being transported upstairs. Amrik Singh and Rajinder got down to plastering the walls. The work had started at eight and was finished by twelve, much ahead of the scheduled time. We washed and changed and returned to our barrack.

On his round of the barracks at twelve Fazaldad was surprised to find us taking it easy in out barrack. "Why, has Shera given you half the day off?" he asked.

"No, Janab, we have finished our day's work," Amrik Singh replied. "You can go and see for yourself if you like."

Fazaldad wouldn't believe him and went to check for himself. The next day he increased the length from 60 to 102 feet. Shera again objected but Fazaldad brushed him aside.

We worked with the speed of lightning and this time too the job was finished by two.

Our efficiency angered Fazaldad; he couldn't bear to see us sitting idle. The next day he asked us to plaster 150 feet of the wall. Amrik Singh was equally annoyed. "Janab, if it irks you to see us sitting idle we shall prefer to work in your presence. We shall have a break from 12 to 2 like other prisoners and then again work from 2 to 5, finishing as much work as we can during this period. Since we shall be going by a time schedule the question of giving an undertaking as to the amount of work we shall handle does not arise."

"I am not concerned at how you go about the job," Fazaldad retorted. "That you must complete 150 feet by evening is all what I'm concerned with."

"No, Janab, we don't have the strength to do so much work," one of us replied. "It's upto you to decide as it pleases you."

Fazaidad snarled at us and went away to fetch a guard to have us beaten up. Shera who had got an inkling of what was going on between us went away to have a word with Superintendent Naseer.

Naseer was on the spot before the guards arrived. On hearing the story he flew at Fazaldad. "It appears you are determined to turn good workers into idlers," he said. "All right, you bring a chair and watch them at work in your presence. None of them will sit idle except for the scheduled break. You can't extract work from them on contract basis. The Jail Manual does not allow it."

The Superintendent went away, leaving Fazaldad standing before us, aghast.

His chair was placed near the 'kot mauka'. He was sitting under the blazing Mianwali desert sun and there was no tree nearby to provide him shade. Within an hour Fazaldad's trousers became wet with sweat and he kept shifting on his haunches. Accustomed to working in office under an electric fan, he was now having his share of the blazing sun which we braved everyday. We could stand the sun, as we were accustomed to hard work but middle-aged Fazaldad wilted under the heat. He seemed to be passing through hell.

Meanwhile Chacha Shera would turn up every hour or so to make sure that Fazaldad had not deserted his post. "I hope you are not feeling the heat," he would ask Fazaldad in jest. In four hours Fazaldad must have called ten times for water. At twelve, he dashed off towards his office, feeling greatly relieved. We had plastered only twenty feet of the wall.

When we resumed the work at two we learnt that Fazaldad had taken leave for the rest of the day. He had got sun-stroke. We again plastered the wall and returned to our barrack. In the evening we learnt that Fazaidad's condition had deteriorated and he was constantly vomitting and purging. In the morning when we reported for work Fazaldad was still missing.

Chacha Shera laughed. "You scoundrels, what have you done to our precious deputy?" he said. "He is on the verge of popping off. Any way, get on to your work. And fix your own targets."

That day we plastered ninety feet till twelve. Fazaldad did not appear for next five days. When he turned up on the sixth day Amrik Singh said, "Janab, may I fetch a chair for you?"

"You bastard stop joking with me," he said "Kot mauka be damned and you along with it! You must have cast some spell on me that I was almost gone for good. I've nothing to do with the likes of you. Let Shera deal with you."

After that we came solely under Shera's charge and didn't see much of Fazaldad. During this period even the nambardars also left us alone and did not pull us up on account of work.

Meeting the Hijackers

I have stated earlier that two Kashmiris, Mohammed Ashraf and Hashim Qureshi had hijacked an Indian plane and brought that to Lahore. Pakistan had celebrated the event with great eclat. They feted the hijackers as they went from town to town. The girls of the Lahore University vied with one another to have them for the night, for they felt proud of the fact that by doing so they were doing honour to the heroes of the nation.

The hijackers made inflamatory speeches at Lahore, Lyallpur, Multan, Montgomery and other towns for liberation of Kashmir. Bhutto gave them an official welcome in the capacity of the President of the People's Party. In spite of India's protest the plane was blown off and wrecked.

The reports of this hijacking and the accompanying photographs made front page news in all the newspapers of Pakistan. In the meantime, Maqbool Butt, the leader of the Kashmir Liberation Front who was undergoing life imprisonment in the Srinagar Jail escaped and joined the hijackers in Pakistan. In retaliation India banned the flights of

Pakistani planes to Bangladesh through the Indian skies. The sea route for the Pakistani ships was also blocked.

In a huff, the Pakistani government laid the blame for hijacking at India's door. The Pakistani government allegedly claimed that it was a part of India's 'Sauce and Cutlet Plan' to deliberately have the plane hijacked to Lahore and blow it up there. This was purposely done to ban the flights of Pakistani aircrafts over India with a view to isolating Bangladesh. It arrested Mohammed Ashraf, Hashim Qureshi, Sardar Maqbool Butt along with his companion Mr Lone and confined them in the Shahi Qila at Lahore for investigation. Here they were severely beaten. Hashm Qureshi was crippled in one arm and Maqbool Butt's leg was damaged, rendering it difficult for him to walk.

The fact is Mohammed Ashraf belonged to the Indian Border Security Force and used to take part in raids on Kashmir organised by Azad Kashmir. Hashim Qureshi was also a member of the same Force. They had planned to hijack an Indian plane in order to put pressure on Indian government to release their comrades from jail.

The government charged them with activities imperilling the security of Pakistan. They were awarded 19 years rigorous imprisonment.

In the course of court proceedings they abused the government and openly declared that the Pakistan government had implicated them in order to save its own skin. They maintained that prior to going into action they had placed the whole plan before the government and obtained its approval. On its part the government had assured them of political asylum. But when it found that things were going against it sacrificed them at the altar of expediency.

These people were imprisoned in the Mianwali Jail. Nobody was allowed to meet them. Qureshi's sister was living in Pakistan. The government had even tried to implicate her and her husband in this case, but according to Hashim, they were able to save their skins by bribing army officers. Ashraf went to the extent of saying that these officers had tried to take liberties with his sister and ultimately she was driven to warming the beds of some of them. It was only then that she and her husband could save themselves from the clutches of the law. Otherwise they too would have been rotting in one of these cells.

One day it rained heavily. Their cells became unfit for habitation. We were still depended upon for the job of repairs of the jail as and when an occasion arose. That day we got on opportunity to talk with them freely.

They told us that the Azad Kashmir government had established secret cells in all important towns of India with the help of CIA. Every year the Azad Kashmir government spent millions of rupees to create political unrest in Kashmir, inciting people against the Indian forces stationed in Kashmir. Through Pakistani pockets they smuggled into Kashmir such material as firearms, explosives, spying cameras, watchlike radio transmitters and propaganda material, including cassettes, calling Indians blood-suckers of the Kashmiris. These cassettes were sent from Pakistan along with tape-recorders. Some of these cassettes were in Urdu and others in Kashmiri. These tape-recorders were distributed free among Kashmiris.

But Kashmiris were a clever lot and could not be hoodwinked easily. They would have fun listening to these cassettes for some time and then they would destroy them for fear of be in caught and sell the American or the Japanese tape-recorders to Indian tourists. The firearms smuggled through Pakistan were also disposed of likewise. They were sold to smugglers also.

According to Qureshi and his friends, there were only a handful of desperadoes fired by the passion of bringing Islamic rule to Kashmir and merging it with Pakistan. They were prepared to do and die to achieve their objective. As for the Kashmiris they were fooling both the governments and thus having the best of both worlds. "Pakistan's callous treatment has embittered us against it," Qureshi asserted, adding, "These people claim that Pakistanis have fooled Kashmiris whereas the fact is that they are the ones who have been fooled by us. It has been going on since the inception of Pakistan. We are prepared to swear by Allah that in Kashmir there is no oppression against the Muslims. Nobody interferes with our religious customs. On the contrary, sometimes we Muslims ride rough shod over sentiments of the Hindus living in

Kashmir. If we believe in the principle of self-determination for the Kashmiris then why don't we restore democracy in Pakistan.

"When we were living in Kashmir, imbued with Islamic passion, we never put this question to the insurgents who came from across the Azad Kashmir border to incite us against India. But if we are given an opportunity to go to their country we would certainly ask them why are they committing such sacrilege against their own countrymen. We have seen mind-boggling things happening there.

"If we go by what we have observed and heard it is not Pakistan but 'Pollutistan' (the land of pollution). God knows I hate to tell lies but believe me when I came to Lahore after hijacking the Indian plane the Lahore University girls flew at one another's throat so as to sleep with me."

I gaped at their faces. These youngmen must have once been so handsome, their faces glowing with health like burnished copper, but now turned sallow because of the unhealthy jail life. And then I thought of those university girls of Lahore who took intoxicating drugs and left the males miles behind in the matter of fashions. It was not surprising if they fell for these daring youth.

I had myself visited the Lahore University several times and knew of girls who were prepared to get out of their clothes for the sake of a cigarette of hemp. So I was inclined to believe what these youngmen had told me.

"What will be your line of action if you were lucky to be sent back to India?" I asked them.

One of them replied: "In the first place I do not have any such hope. No, we may not go back alive from here. But all the same, we have faith in Allah. If we are fated to partake of the food of our country once again we shall certainly find the way back to our country. Then our first task would be to disabuse the minds of our gullible countrymen of Pakistan's false propaganda. We shall unmask the government.

"The present government wants to take over Kashmir to promote the vested interests of a small coterie of people. God forbid, if its dream comes true it would overnight change Kashmir, the so called Paradise on Earth, into a veritable Inferno. There would be no democracy, nor a Kashmiri government. And the present mercenary government of Pakistan would have no scruple in selling Kashmir to the USA or China to enable them to establish their military bases in the lush valleys.

"Even today most of the arms that find their way into Kashmir come from America. Now that China and Russia have no love lost between them, America is left with only one stooge-Pakistan. They can arm it to its teeth and make it fight against India.

"China is already building a road through the Kurakuram Pass and America is establishing a cantomnent at Kharian. Why? Is it to Pakistan's benefit? Far from it. It is doing so in order to lead the Pakistanis towards destruction and establish its Dollar

Imperialism by economically crippling that country."

We were pleased to know their views. It was evident that their hearts had certainly undergone changes.

The repairs on their cells lasted three days and this gave us an opportunity to have a hearty tete-a-tete with them which provided me an insight into the reality of Kashmir for I had never visited that place to know things for myself. Some of the perennial Pakistani propaganda had left its mark on me. I was led to believe that there must be some truth in it. I had wrongly thought that our Indian government was harsh on the Muslims of Kashmir and that was one reason that they were so disgruntled.

Stopover at Lahore – Prelude to Return

Our prison life-style had improved. The days were passing well. We held our sway in prison, having nothing much to do except supervising the work of other prisoners and ordering them about. On the 15th March 1973 we suddenly got the news that our transfer papers were being sent to Lahore. It was said that all the Indian prisoners arrested before 1971 were being assembled at the Kot Lakhpat Jail for exchange.

Our joy knew no bound. We celebrated the news by singing and moving about in jail all night, the Superintendent having graciously agreed to our shackles being removed. We also liberally distributed our stocks of opium and hemp among friends, besides ourselves having a go at them for we thought we would not require them after two days.

The next day in the evening we were put on the Mari-Indus Express on our way to Lahore. This time the guards were all courtesy to us. We kept awake while the guards slept. They knew that we were soon going to be repatriated to out country and hence there was no question of our escaping.

When the train reached the Lahore station we realised that the world had undergone a change. Bell-bottoms had taken the place of narrow pants. The boys, clean-shaved and long-haired, almost looked like girls. Being happy at heart, we found everything agreeable. At that time Major Syyed Bokhari was the Superintendent of the Kot Lakhpat Jail. He had been at Multan in the capacity of the Deputy Superintendent of that jail. He used to be quite brutal with us but in utter contrast, he was quite nice to us at Lahore.

He assembled all the prisoners who had come on transfer in the lawn of the jail and delivered a speech.

"Dear Indian friends," he said, "till now you were imprisoned in Pakistani jails.. But now by orders of the President of Pakistan, Janab Zulfikar Ali Khan Bhutto, your punishment has been revoked and now all of you are with us in the capacity of guests. This jail is now like a transit centre for you. You are no longer prisoners. As the orders come in, we shall, turn by turn, put you on the train and send you to the Wagah border from where you can safely join your families. We shall provide you with necessary stationery so that you can correspond with your people back home. You may go back to your barracks and relax. There were prisoners from other Pakistani jails who have preceded you and there will be more of them coming. I have passed order for new clothes and linen to be issued to you and you will get them soon as you reach your barracks."

We returned to our barracks, where we met many of our

old comrades, one of whom, Abdul Razzaq had been caught in Karachi. He was rather in a bad shape and was admitted into the jail hospital. His knee was swollen and pus had formed in it. Having turned sceptic, his leg had to be amputated to save his life. There were in all four hundred and fifty Indian prisoners assembled there for exchange. Of them, one hundred and ten had gone totally insane, a police inspector from Amritsar being one of them. They had been given so many shocks that their faculty of thinking had become impaired.

There were others who had gone mad because of excessive tortures and still others because of worries. I searched for Khoh Singh, son of Faisla Singh among the lunatics but I could not find him anywhere. I feared that they had either killed him or sent him to Attock Jail under 32B Defence of Pakistan Rules. No Indian bad ever returned alive from that jail.

In the jail we also met Paramjit and Balbir Singh of Ferozpur and Pandit Ashok Kumar of Fazilka. And most conspicuous of all, Amrik Singh who had a big hand in getting many of us arrested. He had sent a petition to the President of Pakistan that he should not be sent to India. He also appealed to the army top brass that in recognition of his services to Pakistan he should be given asylum in Pakistan. It appeared that he was still willing to spy on behalf of Pakistan. Repatriation to India meant sure death for him. All along he was assailed by uncertainty for there was no knowing how India would deal with him. He would come and cringe before me and beg forgiveness for his misdeeds. "I've already been punished for what I did," he would plead. "Please don't depose against me when you return to India."

"Amrik Singh," I would reply, "do you think that our, Intelligetiçe Service is so incompetent as not to have a dossier of your activities in Pakistan? I'll not proceed against you on my own. But if the government questions me I'll be obliged to state the facts as I know them. You have not done me a favour by getting me arrested. The punishment that you have already undergone or will get henceforth is a just retribution for your evil deeds. There's little that I can do about it."

Bangladesh had already come into being. Sheikh Mujib had come to Pakistan to participate in the Islamic Conference. In spite of opposition from within, Bhutto had officially recognised Bangladesh.

We did nothing all day and spent our time playing cards. The notorious smugglers of our country, Ajit Singh Jaul, Gurcharan Singh and Mahinder Singh, all from Amritsar, were with us in jail. Their Pakistani counterparts, equally notorious smugglers, used to meet them right in the Superintendent's office, where fresh deals were struck. Of course the Superintendent had his share in the form of bribes.

The things that these smugglers, who were undergoing imprisonment, got from their friends on their scheduled visits left us astounded – bags of almond, canisters of pure ghee, cartons of imported cigarettes, toothpaste, boxes of perfumed toilet soaps, pure opium, hemp and foreign whiskey. They lived like lords in jail, drank concoctions of ground almond kernels and did jerks to keep themselves in perfect form. They did not have a worry in the world as if they were staying in their father-in-law's house. Not that they kept these thing for their exclusive use; they generously shared them with other prisoners. But only their opium could sell in the jail; none else could make inroads into their territory. The contract for hemp was also with them. They ground *bhang* in the barracks for sale to the prisoners. The prisoners drank it and dozed the whole day in peace.

When the Pakistani prisoners learnt that soon we would be returning to India they tried to socialize with us so that we may carry messages for their friends and relatives in India. They would try to find out an Indian belonging to their erstwhile district in India and urge upon him to meet their relatives. It was for the first time since inception of Pakistan that prisoners were going to be exchanged on such a large scale which also included those hauled up on the charge of spying. As it happened the spies who had been caught in 1953 were still languishing in Pakistani jails. They had not been released even on expiry of their terms.

May God bless Bhutto for keeping his promise us when we were rotting in the cells of Kot Lakhpat remembered it while signing the Simla Agreement in 1972. Jail in Lahore. He had clearly laid down that all Indian prisoners, whether civilian or military, whether spies or smugglers, caught before the 1971 war would be duly exchanged. No exceptions would be made in this regard.

In 1972, when the salient features of the Simla Agreement were announced on the radio we could not believe our ears that such a thing could come to pass. When we started from Mianwaii for Lahore even then many of us were despondent. We only believed it when Major Bokhari delineated the whole thing in so many words, emphasising the fact that we were no longer prisoners. But after that things dragged on for a long time. No further news came down to us as to what was happening.

Then one day all the Indian prisoners were called out and asked to sit in a line. All Of us were, one by one, introduced to a Counsel from the Swiss Embassy. Our home addresses in India were noted down because it had been mutually agreed that all the arrangements for the exchange of prisoners would be made through the Swiss Embassy.

We had already been in Lahore for a year. When we asked the Swiss Ambassador as to when the arrangements would go through he was rather vague about the whole thing and did not come up with any satisfactory answer. He said, "We shall send your lists to the Indian Government who would make necessary enquiries at the respective places where you hail from. When the confirmed lists are in our hands, depending upon the circumstances, we shall effect exchanges in small lots of twenty to thirty from each side. This can take two months and this can as well take two years. I can't hazard any opinion on this point. It all depends on how expeditiously the police of both the countries act."

The Ambassador went away leaving us wallowing in gloom. The exchange could take any length of time for we were familiar with the dilatory ways of the police in both the countries. They never moved until their palm was greased at every step. They would never confirm or testify any statement unless their pocket was lined with money.

In the meanwhile we were finding it difficult to come by cigarettes. We had finished all our stocks before starting from Mianwali not realising that we would endlessly be marking time at Lahore. The cost of living in Pakistan was going up day by day. The Pakistani prisoners were finding it difficult to be generous with their cigarettes and such other treats which were proving a serious drain on their pockets.

The only thing that we could do was to pray that our ordeal should come to an end soon. As the saying goes an idle mind is the devil's workshop. Having nothing to do we would indulge in squabbling. Amrik Singh who was regarded as a traitor of the country came out worst in such encounters. Any excuse would come handy to belabour him.

One day when tie was sleeping in the afternoon some prisoners threw a blanket over him and showered kicks and blows on him. They never gave him a chance to get up. He fainted. Being muffled with a blanket he could not even know who were the persons responsible for giving him such a nice licking. Nor could he lodge a complaint for he had no way of identifying the culprits. He kept crying the rest of the day.

Then he got up and prostrated himself before us. "Kill me, finish me off!" he cried. "I don't want to live. If you can be so callous to me here I shudder to think what fate awaits me in India."

"Son I know your tricks," Chanan Singh Bhuller said. "You want to die to put an end to your misery. But while dying you want to implicate us on the charge of murdering you so that we are retained in Pakistan for the rest of our lives. No, son, we won't let you die like that. We shall kill you by inches. It is after a long time that camel has been entombed under the mountain. We shall not let go of this chance. But first tell me why did you have us arrested? For two thousand rupees, wasn't it? You pimp, if you would have gone to one of the mothers of our prisoners she would have gladly flung two thousand rupees in your dirty face and asked you to let alone her son and act like a man."

Yahya Khan's Sweet-heart

At just about that time the Superintendent of the jail, Major
Syyed Bokhari went away on transfer to some other jail
and his place was taken by Hamid Khan 'Pistol'. This stumpy
five feets six inches tall officer was in the habit of threatening
everybody by saying, "I'll send a bullet through your body"
and had therefore been nicknamed 'Pistol'.

Only after a few days of his arrival, Yahya Khan's sweet-
heart, Begum Aklim Akhtar alias General Rani was brought
to the Lahore jail on remand. General Yahya Khan had just
fallen from power and with his eclipse her authority had also
received a serious setback. She was now having a gay time with
Aziz Ahmed, the director of Pakistan Shipping Corporation.
It is said that one evening General Rani's daughter and another
girl Neel Kamal (I cannot presently recall her muslim name)
were sitting in Aziz Ahmed's lap in his Lahore apartment and
General Rani was sitting across them at a table hilariously
watching the fun over a drink when the police swooped into
their room and arrested her on the plea of indecent behaviour.

She was taken to Naulakha Police Station where she was kept in the lock-up for two full days. Nobody came for-ward to bail her out.

She was in fact the wife of a senior police officer who used her as a means of pleasing his bosses. Once at a private party Yahya Khan's gaze fell on her and she took his fancy. Afterwards he got so infatuated with her that he went all out to have her for himself. Just as Noorjahan's writ ran during Jahangir's reign so did General Rani's during General Yahya Khan's regime; she was the real power behind the General.

Those were the days of Martial Law. Yahya Khan was all in all and there was no one to question his authority. Since General Rani had great influence over Yahya Khan, fortunes were made and unmade at a nod of her head. People trembled at her name. Acting on a whim she could tear off a star from one army officer's epaulet and put it on another's. It was a merry-go-round of promotions and demotions. Nobody dared go against her wishes.

Once a friend taunted her husband, "*Abe O, Saley,* your wife openly goes about with the General." "So what?" the husband replied unabashedly, "Now I've started looking at life more indulgently. I say to myself she's my mistress and Yahya Khan's wife. And it's great, fun to have her on the sly once in a while!" Woe to the country whose rulers and husbands can be so perverse.

From Naulakha Police Station General Rani was transferred

to the Kot Lakhpat Jail. She was lodged in the female ward where one could hear her singing in the stillness of the night. The other women staying in the jail at that time were most of them prostitutes. They sang such bawdy song that even men felt outraged.

With the fall of Yahya Khan she had also fallen from grace and Superintendent Hamid Khan 'Pistol' thought it opportune to take advantage of the situation. He would call General Rani to his office every morning at ten and send her back to the jail at five. She would say in very naked terms, "It makes no difference to a much used skin. Why should I object if this Superintendent can provide me with comforts? I'm a flowing river in which thousands have taken dips!"

The Superintendent would keep her in his office the whole day behind closed doors, leaving his deputy to look after the jail administration. On the days be was required to make a round of the jail he would rush through the ordeal and returning to the office resume his revellery with another bout of drinking holding the Rani is his arms.

One day when the two were having fun together, two prisoners who had a running feud fell upon each other with knives in the jail vestibule. Immediately the alarm was sounded and the Superintendent came out in a burry, buttoning up his trousers. He even forgot to look at his face in the mirror. His cheeks were smeared with lipstick.

"I'll shoot you dead!" he barked at the two prisoners using

his pet phrase, "Why are you creating this rumpus?"

The two prisoners suddenly stopped quarelling as they looked at the Superintendent's face and then laughed. "We quarrel and even knife each other to settle old scores and yet we draw no blood. You don't quarrel and yet your face is red all over. Really, there must be something funny going on." Embarrassed, the Superintendent hurriedly retreated into his office, leaving the jail staff to deal with the prisoners.

Fifteen minutes later General Rani also went away to her cell. But after that to avoid further scandal, the Superintendent stopped calling her to his office.

Though a lot of notoriety had gathered round her name, General Rani was not a bad sort. Generous to a fault and compassionate by nature she would distribute her things among the prisoners and offer milk and fruits to the patients in the jail hospital. There are some personalities who being at cross-purposes with themselves are their own undoing. General Rani was one such person. She used to say, "I offer myself to others at my own sweet will. No one dares touch me against my will and none will in future. Bhutto is now having it out on me because when I was with Yahya Khan he had designs on me and I spurned him. No, I wouldn't let him take any liberties with me. What if the dice is now loaded against me? I'm still General Rani. I may break but I'll never bend. I know this man Bhutto under his skin. He struts about posing big but I know what he is. Wherever he goes be is surrounded by touts, ready with girls for his pleasure. What good can such a man do to his country? The son of a harlot that he is! He did not even spare the wife of Ghulam Mustafa Khar, a man of his own party and the Governor of Punjab. Does the People's Party have no abler man to hold this high office? No, there was a give-and-take behind this move. Soon after Khar's marriage he sent the fellow out for ten days on a foreign assignment and spent that time with his newly wedded wife at the Governor's House at Lahore. Bhutto is a mountebank.

"People, I tell you, are most unpredictable. The time is coming when the mask will be off from this man's face and people will see this mountebank in his true colours. Everywhere people will rise in revolt against him. The hand that had placed him in the President's seat will then go to clutch his throat. The People's Party and its underlings are no better than goondas. They are incapable of running the government. Once again the army will hold the reins of the country and God willing my Yahya Khan will again come to power. Then it will be my day of reckoning. I'll settle accounts with one and all. You just watch and wait. If I don't gun them down publicly by making them stand on the road my name is not General Rani.

"These men have come to power by fooling the people. But my power is based on my youthful charms with which Allah has so bountifully endowed me. A day will certainly come when I'll unmask all those faces. People will spit at their faces and even their wives and daughters will languish in jail."

General Rani's prediction did not prove wrong. Today as I am writing this book newspaper headlines leap up before my eyes. Bhutto's wife Nusrat and his daughter Benazir are both in jail facing trials.

A Conspiracy Against Bhutto

As soon as he gave formal recognition to Bangladesh a storm of protest rose against Bhutto in Pakistan. The Jamait-e-Islam, the Jamiyat-ulema-e-Islam, the Tahreek-e-Istaqlal and even some prominent members of the People's Party turned hostile to Bhutto. President Bhutto, however, dealt with them with a firm hand. He struck terror in their hearts, rendering them infructuous. Besides, what recoiled to Bhutto's advantage was that at that time he was simultaneously holding three high offices in the Pakistan administration -he was the Chief Marital Law Administrator, President (Sadr-e-Pakistan) and its Prime Minister (Wazir-e-Azam).

There was a faction within the Pakistan Army which was not prepared to recognise Bangladesh as a separate political entity. It was in favour of carrying on the war with India with help from America and China. But giving full credence to the prevailing critical situation Bhutto went in for the Simla Agreement with Mrs Indira Gandhi in 1971. Bhutto had realised that following America's advice Pakistan had come to grief in the three wars waged against India in 1948, 1965 and the more recent one in 1971; this particular war had almost broken Pakistan's backbone. Bhutto did not want to invite more trouble by adopting a hostile attitude towards India. Besides, he, had also to think of the 93 thousand Pakistani soldiers and 195 high army officers who were being held as prisoners of war in India.

This was the cardinal factor which had inducd Bhutto, who had bragged in the LJN that Pakistan was prepared to wage a thousand year war against India, to sign the Simla Agreement. The agreement not only helped him get the prisoners released but also regain thousands of miles of Pakistani territory which had been run over by the Indian army.

The anti-Bhutto faction in the Pakistani army soon revealed its hand. General Zia-ul-Haq was the leader of this faction of dissidents and had with him one Brigadier (whose name I cannot presently recall), Col. Asif Shafi of the 2nd Punjab Regiment, Maj. Aiyaz Ahmed Sipra and 122 other officers. They had planned to have Bhutto and his family placed under house arrest at his own residence and by his own security guards. It had also been decided to kill ten lakh adherents of the various political parties.

The meeting where the above plan was being formulated was still in progress when General Zia-ul-Haq observed that the Brigadier was rather luke-warm to the proceedings and was giving perfunctory replies to his questions. Fearing lest the

Brigadier should leak out the whole thing to President Bhutto and get him trapped, he forestalled the Brigadier by himself divulging the whole conspiracy to President Bhutto and holding the Brigadier as the key-figure of the conspiracy. Thus he not only wormed his way into Bhutto's confidence, thereby making his own position secure but also superseded many senior officers to become the Commander-in-Chief of the Pakistani army. 127 army officers were arrested the same night along with the Brigadier. They were straightway taken from their homes to the Attock Jail where they were interrogated which ended in their court martial and long terms of imprisonment. The Brigadier was awarded 20 years' rigorous imprisonment and Col. Asif Shafi seven years hard labour. Likewise the other officers were also sent to various jails. Of them Col. Shafi and Major Aiyaz Ahmed Sipra were lodged in the Lahore Jail where I was awaiting my repatriation to India.

Major Sipra was put in a cell in barrack No. 4 where I used to visit him quite frequently. Such meetings were strictly forbidden but I somehow managed it; a couple of cigarettes to the guard generally did the trick in getting me through to him. Gradually Maj Sipra developed a liking for me and we spent the day together playing cards or chess or just gossiping. Col. Asif Shafi was locked in barrack No. 1. His nambardar was a very strict fellow and would not allow anyone to meet him- not even a Pakistani prisoner. I had only a brief glimpse of him on the Id day when he came to greet Sipra in his cell along with his nambardar.

In the course of our meetings I learnt in great detail from Major Sipra about the conspiracy against Bhutto. Tall and well-built, Sipra hailed from Gujarat (a town in Pakistan), he had a great hatred for India which he expressed in virulent terms. "I call you here just to divert my mind," he would say. "Except you I don't find anyone in this jail to match my mental calibre. All others are no better than yokels – plain illiterate buffoons. Otherwise, I hate the very looks of Indians."

He told me that they had won over the Commander of Bhutto's Security Guard who was to take Bhutto unawares and arrest him along with his entire family while they were having their breakfast. An official proclamation was to be read out to him there and then that he had been removed from power. "But as luck would have it, our own General Haq who had master-minded the scheme betrayed us. We were arrested the same night. It speaks volumes for our integrity that we did not bring in General Haq at any stage in connection with this military coup. We thought that like us he must have also been put under arrest. Hence when the 127 of us were brought to the Attock Jail and we did not find General Zia-ul-Haq there we thought possibly he had been shot dead or that his name had been withheld from Bhutto for some special reason. Little did we know that our own leader had betrayed us."

As I learnt from Sipra, these officers were kept in the Attock Jail for three months where no news from the outside world ever reached them. There were also forty Indian prisoners lodged in that jail, of whom about eight had been there since 1965 and the rest were arrested by the Pakistani army during the 1971 war.

"For all I know they are still there," Sipra continued. "Among them one Capt. Singh and another Gill of the Indian Air Force had become friendly with me. Every day we played badminton together and watched TV. But they are destined to stay there till the very end. Any Indian who once passes through the portals of the Attock Jail never comes out again. Only the *rotis* of the fort fall to his lot and a canister of kerosene on death to burn his dead body. There is no redemption for him as long as he lives.

"At first we thought that we would also meet the same fate – that we would be kept in that fort till we breathed our last. But after court martial when the sentence was read out to me I felt greatly relieved. My sentence was the shortest, extending over three years only. And according to my reckoning I'll be due for release in two and a half years from now.

"Whatever happens to me, I'm sure of one thing: There's no escape for Bhutto," Sipra would say with an air of finality. "The day Zia-ul-Haq is able to have his way he will uproot Bhutto. He may even kill him. Don't I know the man? He is blood thirsty. Once he assumes power nothing on earth short of God can unseat him. I tell you, of all the dictators of Pakistan he would prove to be the most ruthless and autocratic.

"He is so strong-willed that once he has nailed decided on something there is no stopping him. He is so soft-spoken and that one fails to notice his nailed fist. May God that he comes to power. Then *bachchu*, (hannless like a child) we shall deal with you measly Indians right and proper. We shall show you what war means. That will be the last and decisive war between India and Pakistan. Then either you will rule over us or we will rule over you. Either Pakistan will disappear from the map of the world or India, the whole of it, will merge with Pakistan. You will be going home soon, won't you? We shall be coming over in your wake, right at your doorstep and force you to read the *Kaima*. I would say, 'Get up, Karar (a low-bom infidel). It's the *Kalma* or your head!' But I've a hunch, you'll again escape death because of your circumcision. A foolproof certificate of your being a Muslim. Damn it, you'll again get away unscathed!"

I could never make out whether Sipra was saying all this in jest or he really meant it. But considering the turn that the events have since taken I have a foreboding that something serious is in the offing in Pakistan. General Zia-ul-Haq has already executed Bhutto. The world thought that the day Bhutto was executed there would be cataclysmic upheavals in Pakistan; it would be like the eruption of a volcano. But nothing of that sort happened. In fact, China, America and Britain have in a way approved of Zia's action and have encouraged Pakistan to enter the nuclear arms race. On the other hand, America has stopped selling uranium to India while it is making reckless supplies of military hardware to Pakistan.

Zia-ul-Haq, it is said, is at the back of Ganga Singh, the self-styled president of Kbalistan. He is collecting millions of rupees by sending out punjabis to all comers of the world via Bangkok on Khalistan passports. President Regen had invited him to dinner at the White House. He has by now become fabulously rich and is dreaming of buying an island somewhere where he could lay the foundation of Khalistan. All this is an unmistakable pointer to the fact that soon armies are going to clash in this region.

The formal recognition of Bangladesh by Pakistan laid the seeds of the instability of Bhutto's regime. He took many drastic steps to keep his hold over the people. To placate the masses he dismissed 15,000 government employees overnight and sent them back home. To humour the people he even openly berated some ambassadors of other countinues at an important international gathering. His tactics only angered his political adversaries who joined hands to rise in revolt to oust him from power.

Maulana Madudi of Jamiat-ulema-i-Istam, Air Marshal Asghar Khan of Tehrik-e-Istaqlal, Wali Khan the son of Abdul Ghaffar Khan, Mohammed Ali Kasuri and even Bhutto's own close associates such as Ghulam Mustafa Khar turned against him. This encouraged Pir Pigaro of Sind who had a following of fifteen thousand armed men to revolt against Bhutto. The Pakistani jails overflowed with people of the opposite parties. Even girlish-looking college boys courted arrest and found themselves behind the bars where they were treated most brutally.

Hundreds of college students had been clapped into the Kot Lakhpat Jail. At night they were taken out in groups of ten and sex-starved prisoners were let loose upon them. The students would run off screaming only to fall and to be sexually assaulted by the prisoners. The jail would resound with their screams throughout the night. Then their heads would be shaved off and they would be lodged in some other barrack so that they could not tell their comrades about the hell that they had passed through.

This period of torture lasted for a month. There was a quick turn-over, the old students being replaced by new ones. They were the same students who used to pray to god to make, Bhutto the President of Pakistan.

The establishment of Bangladesh had crippled the economy of Pakistan. Previously Pakistan used to export jute and tea to other countries but now those earnings had totally vanished. Prices had gone sky-high. For instance, sugar sold at fifteen rupees a seer and onions at six rupees a seer. A cup of ordinary tea cost one rupee. Dalda sold at eighteen rupees a seer.

The cumulative effect of these was reflected in serious political unrest. Now it was the people of the postal department going on strike and next time it was those of the electricity department. Strikes had in fact become the order of the day. The wardens and other employees of the jail would surreptitiously carry away the jail *rotis* wrapped in cloth to feed their children at home. The quantity or the number of things received by the prisoners from visitors on their scheduled visits had markedly declined. Gram and *gur* had taken the place of soap, toothpastes, sweets and fruits. Only rich homes could afford to send such luxuries to their relatives in prison.

Naturally, these changes were also reflected in our day to day life in jail. If we asked for a cigarette from a Pakistani prisoner he would come out with a blunt 'no'. Or he would ask us to have one puff on his cigarette and no more. They said they were now getting only one packet a week from home. In the end we had again started collecting half-burnt stubs which we smoked carefully.

Exchange of prisoners by then had gone under way. Unfortunately again, at the very outset the prisoners came up against one serious snag. At the time of arrest some of the prisoners had given assumed names and wrong addresses to the Pakistani authorities. The Indian government had refused to accept them and had turned them away from the border, saying that they were not her people. In this manner, of the first three batches comprising 150 people as many as seventy had been disowned and sent back. They were having a miserable existence, cursing the Indian Government for giving them such a raw deal. For days together they went without a cup of tea.

I was more lucky. Every day I visited Major Sipra in his cell and had my cup of tea with him. Every alternate day he gave me a packet of 20 Tonk cigarettes. He belonged to an affluent family and his visitors came loaded with gifts.

One day I got food poisoning and kept vomitting and purging for ten hours at a stretch which made me very weak. I even feared my end had come. Sohanlal alias Karachand, carried me to the jail hospital on his back. Kazi, the chief compounder was very rude to Indian prisoners and would not admit me into the hospital immediately. He relented only when the matter was reported to the Superintendent. I had gone so weak that I lost energy enough even to go to toilet.

I eventually turned the comer and recovered but physically I was still in very poor shape. At last I sent word to Major Sipra through Sohanlal to come to my help. I was particularly in need of milk and fruits to pick up strength, but now even Pakistani prisoners got these things most sparingly and to dole them out to the Indian prisoners was out of question.

Major Sipra promptly gave Sohanlal ten rupees and some fruits. He said, "Tell that Karar that when I come to India I'll have the money back with interest. Why should I leave it? That's what your *Bania* ancestors did with our forefathers."

For the next ten days Sipra regularly sent me milk and fruits. Sohanlal was an opium addict and could not withstand the temptation of buying opium with those ten rupees. He kept the money with him but dutifully passed on the milk and fruits to me every day.

One day Sipra personally came to see me at the hospital. "What have you done with those ten rupees," he asked me. I looked blankly at him and then suddenly realised that Sohanlal must have pocketed the money. "I bought cigarettes with that money," I told him. "Sala!" he gave me an angry look. "Did I give you the money to waste it on cigarettes and further wreck your health? I gave it to you to buy good food so that you could recover fast. You must get well soon. Your turn has come. You'll soon be going back to India. I have just seen the list in the vestibule. Your name is there. Sala, can't you even smile? You may forget me when you get back to India. But don't forget the things I've given you to fatten on. Of course, one day I'll come to fork out their price from *you. Insha Allah! Fazal-e-Khuda!*"

The news had its magic. My illness suddenly disappeared as if it had taken wings. I jumped out of my bed, sought my discharge from the hospital and rushed to my barrack where I conveyed the good news to my friends. There were thirty names figuring in the list. My own and Sohanlal's were there but I had no knowledge about the fate of the other friends.

My clothes were in a most wretched condition. Sipra gave a new set of kurta-pajamas to Sohanlal and got a suit, a tie and a pair of shoes for me. It had become difficult to pass the time for every minute our thoughts went to our homes. When for the next three days the jail authorities did nothing to confirm the news we thought that Major Sipra had spun a yarn just to have some fun at our cost.

But on December 8, 1974 we were officially informed that thirty of us should keep in readiness, for the jail van would call at nine next morning to take us away to the Wagah border for exchange with Pakistani prisoners.

Besides myself and Sohanlal those who were to proceed to the border included Babu Madan Gopal, Chanan Singh Bhuller, Jacob Massih Padre, Anwar Khan, Om Prakash Budhwar and Chetan Singh. They had all been arrested on the charge of spying in Pakistan and had been awarded punishments ranging from ten years and upwards in jail to that of execution by hanging.

Feeling greatly elated at the prospects of reaching home we had spent the night singing and dancing, without a wink of sleep.

I Am Back in India!

December 9, 1974. At four in the morning we hurriedly got ready to leave on our dream-come-true journey. We were tense with excitement – happy at the prospect of re-union with our near and dear ones and were fearful lest we should be turned away at the border for lack of confirmation from our government as to our identities. It was a horrifying thought for in that case we would again have to rot in Pakistan jails for an indefinite period which may extend to the end of out lives. Our fear was not imaginary for we had the example of about seventy prisoners before us who had been disowned by our government for lack of proper data and identification. They were neither among the living nor the dead, and were just languishing in Pakistani jails.

We were called into the vestibule at eight and our belongings were carefully examined. Pakistani jails are a veritable miracle. We had exchanged our Pakistani notes with Indian ones through some smugglers who were undergoing terms in our jail and had hid these currency notes on our persons in a most ingenious manner so that there was no chance of their being discovered. I had round my neck an Urdu translation of the Gita made by Abdul Faizi which I had obtained in the Mianwali Jail during the riots. I still have it with me.

At nine the van started for the Wagah border, carrying the thirty of us. It was a closed van which precluded us from having a glimpse of the outside world. We were unloaded at the Wagah border. About a kilometre away from the boundary line there were crowds on either side of the border who had come to receive their relatives from whom they had been separated years ago. Police had been posted in considerable strength on both sides of the border and there were bands playing.

Our handcuffs were removed and we were taken into a tent surrounded by the police and the CID who had arranged tea for us. First the Pakistani prisoners were to be repatriated, the Pakistani spy, Captain Saadat Hasan Beg being the first on the list. He had been awarded death sentence. His wife and brother had come to receive him and were standing only a few feet away from us. Another Pakistani spy, Mohammed Sadiq who used to sell lottery tickets in Jalandhar was also to be exchanged the same day and his relatives were also standing near me. Saadat Hasan Beg stepped across the border shouting, "Pakistan Zindabad!"

The exchange of Pakistani prisoners continued till four. About 160 of them went over to the other side that day. Representatives of the various Pakistani agencies for whom these spies had worked had come to claim them. They were given two hundred rupees each on the spot and asked to report for duty after a week which they would spend with their families.

At four the exchange of the Indian prisoners got under way. My name was fifteenth on the list. Luckily, till now no Indian had been turned away on the ground of non-identification. When a Pakistani Officer placed me before his Indian counterpart, he asked me my name. I gave him my name. "Welcome. Accepted!" the Principal Indian Officer said. I was thrilled and shouted, "Bharat Mata Ki Jai!" Then I ran towards the tent where the prisoners who had been exchanged prior to me were waiting.

A CID officer stopped me and whispered in my ear, "First meet your father. We have not allowed any one to come here but your father has been in the police with us and we have made an exception in his case."

My father's appearance gave me a jolt. His eyes had sunk with crying and his face was so wrinkled. He embraced me and started crying. "Son, why did you leave us?" he wailed. I had to make an effort to quieten him. He probed and felt every part of my body to make sure that they had not crippled me. I took him into the tent and introduced him to my comrades.

We were told that we could not directly proceed home because in the first batch some Pakistanis had been sent down in the guise of Indians. Hence it was necessary to double check our identity. In my case a Municipal commissioner of our town would be coming over to identify me. My father left for home while we were sent to the Amritsar jail where a camp had been set up to lodge people of our category.

The next day representatives of the various Intelligence Departments came to meet us. They had been entrusted with the job of recording our statements, each representative taking charge of four or five of us. They were particularly required to ascertain how each one of us had first entered Pakistan and about our other credentials. I was surprised to find Subedar Piara Singh Cheema among the investigators, he being none other than the one who had lodged Amrik Singh in my room at Jalandhar. Amrik Singh, it seemed, used to get all his clues through this man to be passed on to the quarters concerned in Pakistan. It was through him that I and five or six of my companions had been apprehended in Pakistan. I quietly brought this fact to the notice of the authorities and the next day I saw no more of Cheema.

It took ten days for the authorities to record our statements and clear us. On the 19th December, Mr Satish Kumar Jain, Municipal Commissioner of Basti Tekanwali at Ferozpur came to our camp in the jail and attested in my favour. My father and Mr Sodhi who lived in the same street with us came to fetch me. I left the jail at six in the evening and we caught a bus for Mukchu from where we took the train for Ferozpur, reaching there at eleven the same night.

A lot of people had come to receive me at the station. They had brought my wife Prabha with them decked as a bride. At the station I was swamped under garlands. Throughout the night our house wore a festive look as if we were celebrating a wedding. The girls clapped and danced as they do at weddings.

Our house looked so different from what it used to be when I was last here. In the last seven years it had not even – been white-washed and plaster had peeled off from the walls. The bricks now exposed to view were a witness to the privations my aged parents had undergone in my absence from home.

Right on the 9th December there was a telegram from Dr Harivansh Rai Bachchan sent to my mother from Bombay : "Rejoice Mohanji's arrival."

Soon after my arrival I wrote him a letter in reply.

In another letter, congratulating me on my new lease of life he urged me to record my experiences in Pakistan in the form of a book – This book which you now find in your hands was inspired by Dr Bachchan.

The Aftermath

For some days there was an unending stream of visitors to our house. Many came from far off places out of curiosity; they wanted to have a look at me and asked me all sorts of questions. I had made adequate arrangements to serve tea to the visitors at all odd hours for which the kettle was kept boiling all the time. But soon the euphoria wore off, the stream of visitors dwindled and the problem, "What should I do for a living?" started haunting me in its brute nakedness. True, people had been of great help to my family in my absence. But now that I was back, my self-respect would not allow me to live on the crumbs of others. But before I could find my bearings or approach the government for help Emergency was clamped on the country. On the 16th march, 1977, when Smt. Indira Gandhi came to Ferozpur to make a speech at an election compaign, a horde of erstwhile prisoners repatriated from Pakistan came from far-flung places at my instance to participate in a huge procession.

In the General Elections of 1977 Mrs, Indira Gandhi lost

conclusively and the Janata Government came to power. Since we were in straitened circumstances, we decided to meet all the high officials of the government at the Centre and even the ministers, pleading for help. Every one of them would accept our memorandum, glance through it and then forget about it for good the moment our backs were turned on them. Fortunately for me, I had done my B.Ed. and I managed to get a teacher's job in a school on the basis of my experience and past reputation but for which I would have been going from door to door with a beggar's bowl.

The various political parties which had formed the Janata Goverment held a conference at Delhi in May 1977 which I attended as a delegate from Ferozpur. On this occasion I sought an interview with the then Prime Minister, Shri Morarji Desai and I met him accompanied by my elder son, Jhalkeshwar Bhaskar. I pleaded with Moraiji Desai that the Indian Government should adequately compensate the Indian nationals who had rotted in Pakistani jails and had sacrificed their lives for their motherland. The reply that I got from Moraiji even today gives me a tail-spin.

If at that time I had a pistol with me I would have kept firing till I had exhausted all the bullets from its chamber, so incensed was I at his reply. His reply was: "Why should we suffer for your mistakes commited in Pakistan? Do you mean to say that if Pakistan government had kept you in jail for twenty years then our government should have compensated you for the same number of years?"

The man who had delivered this oracle had spent nineteen months in jail during the Emergency and in the name of 'atrocities' committed on him during this period of incarceration he had staked his claim to the Prime Ministership of India. Not only that he had also introduced a pension scheme for all the other members of his party who had been in prison with him for nineteen months.

What roused my ire was that I had personally known this man. He had written me scores of letters prior to 1967 which were still with me. But I burnt most of them in anger for what he had said that day.

Some stray ones are still left with me. In one of them he had gone on to the extent of suggesting that he won't mind the changing the date of the meeting already fixed, to suit my convenience.

That very day I said my last goodbye to the Janata Party and its ignominous leader, Morarji. Thanks to my own enterprise and the help of my friends, my financial condition had by now considerably improved. Today I have no complaint against my motherland nor against the Indian government. But even so, when I look at the plight of some of my comrades I am moved to tears.

According to the Fundamental Rights provided by our Constitution every Indian citizen has the right to raise his voice against corruption under the 'right against exploitation'. Today taking protection under that right I maintain that in the name of patriotism we are playing with the lives of thousands of young men. Some of them are lured into this hazardous profession of spying for lack of employment and get nothing out of it. All they get is the enemy's bullet as soon as they cross the border. Those who escape the bullet have to face unending torture and indescribable humiliation in the enemy's jail. It leaves me in wonderment that our urine-drinking erstwhile Prime Minister Morarji Desai had the gumption to fete and laud for three days such notorious smugglers as Haji Mastan, Bakhia and the shipping magnate Dharam Teja – all who had tinkered with crores of rupees – but he had no time even to say a word of sympathy for those people who had staked their lives for the country, spent their days in death cells and faced unimaginable brutalities in the enemy jails.

Nevertheless, I am grateful to my country which saved me from the jaws of death and gave me a new lease of life.

The truth is that I have not done any favour to my country. I have only done my duty by it. I only feel peeved when people posing as patriots fly over our heads and drive past us in limousines. They disappear after making high-sounding speeches which are no more than empty words. They smear their little fingers with blood and pass for martyrs while those who shed their blood for the country are ignored and pushed aside. How long will these hypocrites keep fooling the people? It is time that their bluff was called.

If in the heat of passion I have said something bitter and hurt anybody's feelings I crave his forgiveness. Everybody's except Morarji Desai's. I would rather keep him out of it.

Thank you!